ADVANCE PRAISE F
MUSLIM AMERICAI

MW01096333

Muslim American Writers at Home is a compelling compilation that sheds light on the lived experiences of Muslims from diverse backgrounds, living in Canada and the U.S. Works like this are especially important in our current times as it is critical that Muslim artists take ownership of their own stories and narratives.
– GAMA (Gathering All Muslim Artists)

These authentic, diverse and multidimensional voices lift "layers of ignorance" about Muslims and Islam as they take us beyond and beneath the mainstream, fake narrative. Interweavers of creativity and spirituality, these Muslim authors, whether born in, brought to, or fled to North America, take us to their "real" world of being "racialized, minoritized, and thus dehumanized," via firsthand story-tellings of lived experiences, as we forge ahead toward understanding, faith, love, peace and justice, inshallah. An insightful, painful, impressive, hopeful read.
– Laila Hasib, Inked Resistance Islamic Publishing

At times heartbreaking and beautiful, and at times raw and unvarnished, this worthy anthology provides non-Muslim readers with the perfect antidote to the stereotypes that pervade popular media. This collection contains true gems.
– Graeme Truelove, author of *Un-Canadian: Islamophobia in the True North*

In these times, with bigotry forcibly colliding with visions of a fresh, free and just future, Valerie Behiery's, Hanan Hazime's and Kitty Costello's absolutely marvelous and compelling *Muslim American Writers at Home* is an essential contribution. Writers, of course, are known primarily by their writing, and practicing Muslim writers carry the burdens and blessings of their beliefs, whether or not those are expressed in their work. Here we get intimate glances at their lives, their principles, attitudes, and habits, their experiences of migration and more. Here we can begin to understand what is human and common among us, a vital step toward liberation from prejudice and stereotype, toward belonging and acceptance. And that step, in these times, is absolutely critical. – Jennifer Heath, author of *Extraordinary Women of Islam* and *The Veil: Women Writers on Its History, Lore, and Politics*

This anthology gives voice to diverse Americans and Canadians whose identities include being Muslim. These writings are moving, powerful, and a celebration of our common humanity. It is not a book to be read once and then stored on your library shelf. Rather, these stories should be shared and discussed with others so as to develop a greater understanding of the life experiences of North American Muslims.
– Alia Hogben, Former Executive Director of the Canadian Council of Muslim Women.

Home. Where is it exactly? Is it our childhood house, village, our grandmother's kitchen? Could it be the call to prayer ringing out from the local mosque? Is it the fan that whisks away the oppressive heat as we lay on our bed ? Could it be the smell of fresh pineapple? Or the fragrance of olives in the middle of the harvest? Perhaps it is the scent of jasmine flowers, as we remember being wrapped in warm towels after our bath? Or could it be the bright clean cold snow of our new village. Perhaps it is the homeless man on the street in LA, who calls out to us words of caring and encouragement as we walk by, clearly from somewhere else. Maybe it is the sign that says, "Love trumps hate." In this beautiful collection of poems and essays, we are taken on a journey to find "home" and, ultimately, acceptance and belonging, a shared humanity, through tears and laughter, through strength and fortitude.
– Helen Zughaib, visual artist, author of *Stories My Father Told Me*

Muslim American Writers at Home is a vibrant collage of experiences and emotions. Some pieces will wrap you in their soothing warmth, others will snatch away your blanket of comfort and thrust you into the harsh reality where home and identity are only chaotically defined. As a Muslim American, I am always comforted to learn that I am not the only one whose tongue gets tied when I'm asked, "Where are you from?" I am comforted to learn that I am not the only one who is sometimes made to feel like an outsider in my home country. And that, although I look the part, I do not fit coherently in my parents' home country either. I am always comforted to learn that others carry their homes with them as well, in their hearts, in their families. The pieces in this collection display all of these perceptions, and so much more. With accomplished eloquence, they unveil the rich diversity of Muslim Americans while simultaneously featuring the thick ropes which meld us together as Muslims, as Americans, and most importantly, as humans. This collection of stories, essays, and poems will remain a timeless legacy not only for the writers themselves, but for all of us who identify as Muslim Americans... in whichever form that identity may take.
– Hend Hegazi, author of *Normal Calm, Behind Picket Fences*, and *Even in the Breaks*

These powerful, poignant, personal stories about being a Muslim in North America make for a compelling and very readable collection – one that cries out for our attention. – Linda McQuaig, Canadian journalist & author

MUSLIM AMERICAN WRITERS AT HOME

Stories, Essays and Poems of Identity, Diversity and Belonging

Edited by Valerie Behiery,
Kitty Costello and Hanan Hazime

FREEDOM VOICES

San Francisco, CA, USA

© 2021 Freedom Voices and the individual authors and artists.

Layout and cover design by Aquil Virani
Cover art by Shae Stamp and Aquil Virani

P.O. Box 423115
San Francisco, CA 94142
www.freedomvoices.org
books@freedomvoices.org

Distributed to the trade by:
AK Press, 370 Ryan Ave. #100, Chico, CA 95973; akpress.org

Acknowledgements • Mahin Ibrahim's piece, "How I Found Love from My Homeless Neighbors" was originally published in *Fury: Women's Lived Experience during the Trump Era*, edited by Amy Roost and Alissa Hirshfeld, Regal House Publishing, 2020. • Reem Sayem el Dahr-Hammad's piece, "Jasmine" was originally published in the anthology, *Sisters Singing: Blessings, Prayers, Art, Songs, Poetry and Sacred Stories by Women*, edited by Carolyn Brigit Flynn, published by Wild Girl Publishing, 2008. • Alternate versions of Leena Barakat's and Duraid Musleh's interviews were published and displayed in Najib Joe Hakim's "Home Away from Home: Little Palestine by the Bay" Project, 2015, which featured San Francisco Bay Area Palestinian Americans in photographs, and in recorded interviews about their sense of home. • Tehmina Khan's poem, "Words for a Distant Grandfather," was originally published in *Poets 11: an anthology from the San Francisco Poets 11 reading series,* selected by Jack Hirschman, 2008. Her poems, "4 Boxes," "Ode to Tea," "Passion," "Words for a Distant Grandfather," and her essay, "Love in Dark Times," were previously published in her chapbook, *Ammam's Photo Album and other Poems,* 2017.

Artwork & Photographs • Page 30: Photos by Aquil Virani, Unknown • Page 118, 119, 122: Drawings by Katie Miranda Al Ali

Library of Congress Control Number: 2020950028
ISBN: 9780915117321

Printed in the United States of America

"*Your task is not to seek for love, but to find all the barriers within yourself that you have built against it.*"

— **Jalâluddîn Rumi**

I'm Sorry/I Forgive You (Diptych),
2012, digital print, 76.2 x 101.6 cm
(each). Reproduced with the kind
permission of the Abouon family.

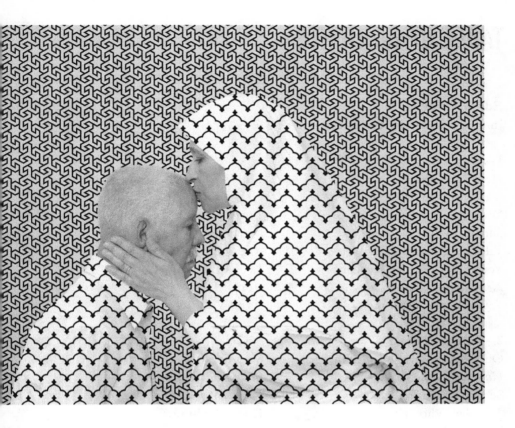

IN LOVING MEMORY OF
ARWA ABOUON (1982 – 2020)

Editor's note: The couple featured in *I'm Sorry/I Forgive You* are the late artist's parents. Family relationships are a central focus of Arwa Abouon's art, and it is indeed rare to see such loving representations of Muslims. The work only increases in emotional power when viewers learn that these images were conceived and produced while her father was suffering from cancer, to which he later succumbed. *I'm Sorry/I Forgive You* is one of Arwa Abouon's most appreciated works.

TABLE OF CONTENTS

EDITORS' PREFACE

Our original call for manuscripts for this anthology invited North American Muslim writers to submit works on themes of identity, ancestry, immigration, home and more. We received submissions from Canadian and U.S. Muslims, including one Latinx Muslim writer. At least 75% of the submissions came from women, and as a result, the book contains a majority of writings by women.

We organized the selections into the following seven sections:

Shoutout —— calls out the many ways the writers have felt welcome or unwelcome in America. These pieces are sassy, funny, moving, grateful, in your face – about the ways these writers have felt misunderstood, maligned, and attacked, or on the other hand, warmly welcomed and included, sometimes by small acts or words of kindness, sometimes by allies who stand up and speak out strongly in their defense.

Finding Home —— shows us the amazingly diverse identities of Muslim Americans. Indian American, American Indian, Palestinian, Puerto Rican, Ugandan American and more, these Muslim writers descend from an astonishing interweave of cultures, languages and ethnicities, and pioneer through uncharted multiple identities, always being asked, "Where are you from?" One piece is entitled *Hiraeth,* a Welsh word meaning: homesickness for a home to which you cannot return, or for a home which may never have been. This longing permeates many of these pieces.

Home Is Here ——— features the voices of North-American-born Muslims, voices that range from first-generation converts to Muslims with ancient family roots. For some, their families have been here for centuries, arriving as Puritans on the Mayflower or arriving as enslaved Africans who had to hide their Muslim faith. They embody dignity, pride and resilience as they weather anti-Muslim ignorance and prejudice, sometimes from within their own families, and create a life filled with purpose and belonging.

Blood Harmonies ——— sings of family ties. Here we find stories and poems about parents, grandparents, children, spouses and more. These tributes, portraits, memories, laments, and dreams are interwoven with the complexities of the immigrant experience, the desire to maintain religious and cultural identity, as well as the inevitable American fusion experience, which can both separate and unite the generations.

The Home I Left ——— tells tales of "the Old Country," portraying some of the enduring relations and identities that remain with these writers in their newfound home. In Palestine, Pakistan, Tunisia, the Arabian Gulf, we are steeped in the sensual delights and sometimes jarring new realities of homes that were left behind, and we meet some of the loved ones who still live there.

Under the Blue Tent ——— speaks to and from the point of view of children and teens, including one nine-year-old Muslim poet. We meet a feisty tomboy and a young inventor falsely accused of being a terrorist. We see through the eyes of a teen whose family migrates to a metaphoric land where prejudice prevails. We see the vast blue sky as "Allah's blue tent" we all live beneath. And we hear from a Muslim mom who has created and published her own children's stories so that Muslim children can see themselves represented.

Ocean of Humanity —— overflows with mythic and poetic ponderings, praises and prayers, inviting us to sip our tea in communion with all people of the world, or sip our coffee as a doorway to ancient identity and divinity. We celebrate the original women of Islam, and find ourselves pondering what may result from our good deeds after we die, with the encouragement to do more good while we are still here. We are asked how we can keep faith in humanity despite its "naked wounds," then invited to "unfasten your cluttered mind" and bow in prayer.

Among these rich and diverse voices, dozens of languages from around the world are spoken, and you will likely find words here that are new for you. We have chosen to italicize most non-English words that are not in common usage, and we have included a glossary in the back of the book, with translations of many of the non-English words. You will also notice variations in the way English words are spelled— such as centre and center, empathise and empathize, neighbour and neighbor. These differences generally reflect the individual author's Canadian or U.S. background, and we have intentionally included both variations.

We acknowledge that we have privileged English in this text by making it the reference point for other languages, and we are grateful to the authors, especially the many French-speaking Canadians and Arabic speakers, for offering this bridge and education to English-language readers.

AN INTRODUCTION IN THREE VOICES
1 — HANAN HAZIME

Putting together this anthology has been a labour of love for myself, Dr. Valerie Behiery, and Kitty Costello, and we hope that you will be as moved and inspired as we were by all the stories, poems, and personal essays. As a Muslimah writer and writing instructor based in Toronto, I am continuously working towards the empowerment of Muslim voices, so when Valerie approached me about being an editor for this anthology, I immediately said yes. I believe there is a dire need for Muslim Americans to fully and authentically express themselves and their experiences in the face of today's widespread Islamophobia. As long as our stories are not heard, we will continue to be 'othered,' dehumanized, and reduced to two-dimensional stereotypes. Also, representation matters. It is necessary for Muslim Americans to see themselves reflected in literature because, according to Dr. Nicole Martins, an American Media professor, symbolic annihilation "is the idea that if you don't see people like you in the media you consume, you must somehow be unimportant." However, we are important and our voices must be given the recognition they deserve.

To my Muslim sisters and brothers, I hope that you will see yourself represented in the pages of this anthology, *Insha'Allah*.

To my non-Muslim sisters and brothers, I hope that this anthology presents you with the opportunity to see a side of Muslims that differs from the dominant racist and orientalist discourse around Islam/Muslims and that challenges the mainstream western media's stereotypical, one-dimensional portrayal of Muslims.

And to all readers, both Muslim and non-Muslim, before you delve into the wonderful reading journey that awaits you, I hope that you can take a moment to be mindful of any preconceived notions of what you may think writing by Muslims entails. This is an anthology that consists of diverse and authentic Muslim voices, voices you may not have heard before. You may find yourself learning about new perspectives and ultimately discovering that the lived experiences of Muslim Americans are infinitely pluralistic.

Unfortunately, contemporary Western discourse often essentializes the experiences of Muslims and ubiquitously represents all Muslims as either being oppressed victims of Islamic theology or radical terrorists who condone violence in the name of Islam. Instead of focusing on the rich diversity of Muslim stories, many mainstream narratives about (or even by) Muslim Americans often focus on the alleged "oppressive nature" of Islamic cultures and theologies. For instance, if you walk into an American book shop and find a book about the hijab or Islamic veil, you will discover that in most cases, the hijab is portrayed solely as an object that oppresses and subjugates women. Even progressive spaces with good intentions often contribute to the essentialization of Muslims by solely representing Muslim individuals as being universally oppressed victims of Islamophobia and racism. We are shown either as terrorists instigating oppression, or as being oppressed by our own religion/culture, or oppressed by Islamophobia. Muslims are often not given the chance to simply exist as multidimensional humans.

The mainstream western media constantly politicizes Muslim bodies, experiences and struggles. We are consistently othered and dehumanized. Despite the fact that many Muslim Americans are not of Arab or South Asian descent, mainstream media/literature insists on depicting Muslims exclusively as Arab or South Asian. Muslim Americans who do not fit these identities or stereotypes may find their lived experiences and "Muslimness" questioned. It is often expected that as a Muslim-American writer you will directly address themes such as Islamophobia, oppression, terrorism, cultural assimilation and/or other contemporary political issues in your work.

In fact, my own literary work has been, at times, met with criticism and disapproval in certain progressive literary circles for not being "Muslim" or "Arab" enough. If I am not exploring the aforementioned themes in my work, my Muslim identity is put on trial. For instance, I have been working on a magic realist story about a mermaid living off the east coast of Canada. Although the story mainly explores themes of sexuality and madness, the feedback I have commonly received has been that I need to more explicitly explore race, religion, gender, and their corresponding modes of oppression. Never mind that my story has nothing to do with racism or Islamophobia. Simply being Muslim and Arab somehow necessitates that my work centre itself around those identities, completely disregarding any intersectionality. Never mind that my character is Canadian and would most likely prefer eating *poutine* over raw *kibbeh* (a type of Lebanese meat tartare); her hyphenated identity unfortunately invokes biased stereotypes about what it means to be a second-generation Canadian immigrant.

On the other hand, less progressive literary circles will often dismiss my literary work altogether if it favourably explores anything remotely related to Islam. My narrative of an empowered Canadian *Muslimah* feminist who chose to wear hijab is not one that matches the mainstream discourse and as such is often rejected and not given space to be heard. Erasure of Muslim voices that don't fit the mainstream narrative and glorification of Muslim voices that do is not okay. Equal representation of diverse Muslim voices is not only more inclusive, it is absolutely vital.

By dictating what kind of narratives by/about Muslim Americans are privileged and disseminated, both progressive and non-progressive media can be problematic and represent Muslims inauthentically. However, I hope that once you read this book, you will have an authentic and heterogenous snapshot of a vast array of Muslim-American experiences and stories.

You will find that not all the works in this anthology explicitly depict experiences of Islamophobia or oppression. While some of the writers have directly addressed issues like Islamophobia or racism in their pieces, other writers have penned stories and poems sharing lived experiences that go beyond the scope of Islamophobia-induced trauma and oppression. Sometimes, we just want to write about chocolate cake or jasmine flowers, or in my case, a magic realist story about mermaids. We are multifaceted human beings with intersectional identities and a plethora of varied experiences, including struggles with Islamophobia, racism, and cultural assimilation, but those struggles don't encompass our existence entirely. With this in mind, I would like to share with you my poem, "Introduction to Poetry by a Muslimah Poet" (after Billy Collins' poem "Introduction to Poetry") in hopes that you take the spirit of its message into consideration while reading the anthology.

I hope that you approach these works with an open mind, an open heart, and a willingness to empathize with stories that may be very different from your own. Assalamu Alaykum.

— *Hanan Hazime,*
Toronto, Canada, 2020

INTRODUCTION TO POETRY
BY A MUSLIMAH POET

I ask them to take my poem
and slowly unfurl its intricate layers
like a blooming tea flower

or press an ear against its pulsing heart.

I say deep dive into my poem
and explore its shadowy crevices,

or shine a light on the poem's surface
and watch as its iridescent metaphors dance.

I want them to take an evening stroll with my poem,
and invite it to Sunday brunch with their mothers.

I want them to cradle my poem in their arms,
and sing it to sleep under the moonlight.

I want them to bring my poem to their lips,
and savour its diverse, delectable flavours.

But all they want to do
is tie my poem to a chair with rope
and smother it in "exotic" spices
—curry, saffron, turmeric.

They want to slather it in hummus,
make it taste more "Muslim."

They begin stabbing my poem with pitchforks
to find out where it's *really* from.

AN INTRODUCTION IN THREE VOICES
2 – KITTY COSTELLO

This anthology was conceived of by artist, writer, and teacher Valerie Behiery, who has long used her own creative work to promote a deeper understanding of Muslim culture, beyond the shallow and stereotyped images that dominate western media. Valerie and I met in an online writing class in 2018, and when she heard that I work with Freedom Voices Publications, whose mission is to "publish works that speak to and from communities on the margins," she reached out to propose this collaboration, the book you now hold in your hands. That is how the book was born and how a non-Muslim like me came to work on this project. We soon invited in the multi-talented artist and poet Hanan Hazime to round out our editorial team.

My trajectory toward this unexpected collaboration was sparked as I witnessed the upwelling of Islamophobic attacks in the U.S. and wished I could do something besides just giving money to the American Civil Liberties Union and wailing about our heartless president. In 2017, as shockwaves of bigotry were mounting across America, I had the following conversation with an old friend, a staunch feminist:

She wondered, "What will we do if they start rounding up Muslims like they did with the Japanese?"

I answered off the top of my (bare) head, "We'll put scarves over our heads and go stand with them en masse, so the police can't tell who's who."

My friend: "How can you suggest that? Those head-coverings are horrible symbols of women's oppression! That's ridiculous."

Me: Silence and confusion…

I was rankled by what she said, while at the same time, I burned with my own ignorance that left me empty of helpful words. And when I looked around to take stock of my friendships and alliances, I saw how few Muslims there were in my life… until I met Valerie. That is where my gentle schooling began. As a middle-class, educated, straight,

English-speaking white woman, raised as a Catholic in the U.S., and as a lifetime social justice advocate, I needed and wanted an education. I share with you here a few of the lessons I am learning, lessons that may be helpful for my fellow good-hearted, unschooled, non-Muslim Americans to know, and may bring a smile to Muslim readers. But first a vignette…

In the online writing class where Valerie and I met, she was the one writer who did not post a picture of herself; she posted a lovely plant image instead. So she and I began working together on this book before I ever laid eyes on her. Shortly into our collaboration, I wrote to her in an exchange that went something like this—

Me: "Valerie, I want to ask you a question, but it hurts my heart to have to ask you this. When we were in the writing class together, did you not post a picture of yourself because you wear a hijab? Did you think we'd be prejudiced if we saw you in a hijab?"

Valerie: "First of all I want to say, feel free to ask me anything. It's how we build bridges. Second, yes. It's true. I wear a hijab, and I thought the other writers might be prejudiced because of it."

Lesson #1: Wearing a hijab in America can be that hard. And Lesson #2: Building bridges can be that simple—curiosity and care on one side, openness and trust on the other—these are things Valerie had faith and vision to foresee.

The next lesson came when I told Valerie about my conversation with my super-feminist friend, the one who was incensed that I would suggest donning a hijab in solidarity with Muslims. When I referred to my friend as an ardent feminist, Valerie said quietly, "I'm a feminist." Simple as that, lesson #3: There are many feminist heads under hijabs.

Then as submissions came in and the three of us collaborated from afar on selections and edits, I sat all by myself at my laptop and received a world-class awakening. Layers of ignorance were ever-so-graciously and eloquently overturned by reading the words of my Muslim brothers and sisters. I practiced speaking aloud names and words I've never heard before, rolling them around in my mouth. I 'met' my first Native American Muslim and my first Puerto Rican

Muslim. I found out (how did I not know?) that many Muslims were brought to the Americas from Africa as enslaved people, smuggling their religion with them. I felt in my core what it can do to you to be seen as a perpetual suspect. I was privy to and a bit envious of the gracious greetings and blessings Muslims so often bestow upon each other when they meet. I was intrigued to learn that because Ramadan goes by the lunar calendar, over the course of years, it gravitates through the seasons—sometimes Ramadan at the height of harvest; sometimes Ramadan in the dark of winter, and so on.

And here are a few more major lessons: I came to understand that the near disappearance of the hijab in so many Middle Eastern and African countries during the early 20th century was largely the result of colonialism and of western pressure on Muslim cultures to assimilate into western looks and values. Though many women did voluntarily or defiantly remove their hijabs, many Muslim women in recent times have voluntarily or defiantly donned the hijab to reclaim their indigenous dress, as well as giving needed support to their chosen spiritual path. That is not to ignore the fact that there are many women who live without human rights and are forced to dress in a particular way, and we oppose those abuses in all their manifestations. But I came to understand that donning modest garb does not mean you are oppressed or brainwashed; it does mean you have to deal with hordes of people who annoyingly assume you are a pitiable, misguided victim.

These writings also teach us how mind-blowingly vast and diverse Muslim American identity and culture are—from Mi'kmaq Muslims to Muslims whose ancestors came on the Mayflower; from Tunisian-Canadians to Puerto Ricans to Irish-American Muslims inspired to convert by reading Malcolm X. But amidst the diversity, there is unity. No matter whether the writer is Muslim-born or a convert, immigrant or American-born, a seasoned elder or a budding young poet, each writer invites us to fall in love with their humanity. As one piece proclaims, our blood, the same color! And we are reminded how even the smallest acts of kindness or welcome can be hugely heartening, and how having support from allies can give Muslim writers and activists the courage they need to go on standing strong.

After reading the illuminating stories and poems so graciously offered by these authors, and helping to bring their writings out into the world, it seems only fair to say something about my own spiritual background and practice and how it has shown up in my work on this anthology. I grew up in an Irish Catholic family in the Washington, DC area, and though I have not been a practicing Catholic in my adult years, I consider myself to be forever "culturally Catholic." I moved to San Francisco in 1977 because it seemed like the most progressive, creative, diverse and tolerant place in the U.S., and I have lived here among its many rich, spiritual and cultural communities ever since.

Over the years I fell into meditation practice, embracing the teachings of the Buddha as a most excellent way to understand the workings of my own mind and behavior, and to learn how to cause less suffering for myself and others. Like Muhammad, the Buddha extolled the virtue of generosity. He said that one of the most important gifts we can give each other is "the gift of fearlessness," described in his words as "the giving of protection to beings when they have become frightened on account of kings, thieves, fire, water, enemies, lions, tigers, other wild beasts, dragons, ogres, demons, goblins, etc." Clearly we are in times like these; we have all been confronting ogres, fire, and more, and so many need protection. I approached this project thinking I might offer the gift of fearlessness to my Muslim brothers and sisters who are speaking up and speaking out. What I found was a great and beautiful irony—that these Muslim writers, who are subject to such prejudice and threat, are speaking words that can bring the gift of fearlessness to me and to us all. When I see their wisdom and courage, I find my own.

I am delighted to have been given this opportunity to hand the microphone to North American Muslims so they can speak for themselves. For the Muslims who contributed to and read this book, may you find rich connection, illumination and mirroring in your loving and diverse community and beyond. For readers who have had little personal connection with or knowledge of Muslims in America, may this book open your heart and mind as it did for me. May it help cure ignorance and build bridges. May we all share in giving the gift of fearlessness to one another.

— *Kitty Costello,*
San Francisco, USA, 2020

AN INTRODUCTION IN THREE VOICES
3 – VALERIE BEHIERY

Creative and spiritual expression have always been interwoven for me. In 1980 at age nineteen, I received a summer scholarship to study modern Greek at the University of Thessaloniki. I was thrilled, not only because I loved to travel, but because I was enamoured with Early Christian and Byzantine art at the time and was eager to explore these *in situ,* beyond textbooks and slides. In fact, when I first flew to Greece, I took a circuitous route through Italy to visit Ravenna, the once Byzantine capital, to experience its formidable glittering gold mosaics, including during a mystical, candlelit concert.

Another time, flying from my home in Canada to Athens, my plane passed through Madrid. Having a few hours stopover, I impetuously taxied in to the Prado Museum to see the paintings of El Greco, one of my favourite artists then. Being the only visitor in the El Greco room and feeling overawed by the power of his art, I remained there for the whole two hours I had. As in all European art, the painter depicts Mother Mary wearing what we now generally refer to as a hijab. Having grown up in a practicing Catholic family, the Virgin Mary's headscarf never bothered me. I hardly noticed it in that my focus was elsewhere, on her story, her soul, or her motherhood.

Perhaps it was the fact that the headscarf formed part of my earliest spiritual imaginary, or perhaps it was simply that Jesus' directive to love one another held my focus, explaining my non-focus and non-concern with the now allegedly contentious piece of cloth. I had the same reaction when I first saw visibly Muslim women. At university in the late 1970s, there was a group of girls from Bahrain who wore the hijab. I did not know them although we said hello and, strangely enough, what I remember observing about them was how they seemed to exude a confidence that I myself was seeking at that difficult age of individuation.

A decade later, as an art teacher, I had students with veiled mothers. And while I still did not see them as 'others,' social and media discourses around Islam slowly cleared my rose-coloured glasses and helped me understand what these Muslim students and parents were going through. I remember sweet, gifted Fatoumata who asked me to 'cook' the plate she painted in class, as they did not have an oven at home, and she wanted the colours to set. In sum, I grew from a world view based on our favourite religion class song in primary school— "*Aimons-nous. Aimons-nous les uns les autres comme dieu nous aime.*" (Let's love one another. Let's love one another just as God loves us.)—to the real world in which whole communities were racialized, minoritized, and thus dehumanized.

As a young struggling artist, I lived for a year or two in a building in which all my neighbours were of North African or African origin. I became particularly close with my next-door neighbour, Bayah, who would invite me in regularly to sit on the floor and eat couscous or to read her mail to her. I knew little about Islam then, and we never discussed it much; we were simply neighbours who enjoyed each other's company. All of the families were busy trying to survive in difficult circumstances. I was, for example, the only one on my floor who had my own bathroom; the rest shared the one at the end of the hall! The kind neighbourhood Arab shopkeepers would let me cumulate bills for my groceries and pay when I could. In short, my lived experience with Muslims forged my personal views, unlike the views of those who feed on mainstream, often-biased headlines.

On a spiritual level, I was passionate at the time—unlike a lot of my generation—about finding the transformative power I was seeking in my native religion. Christianity is embedded in my DNA as a living, powerful transgenerational memory, but two things hindered me. One, I believed Jesus (peace be upon him) when he said in the scriptures that he did nothing except by the will of God his Father, which made it difficult for me to equate him with the Creator. And two, in light of my need for psychological well-being and spiritual growth, I needed a specific daily spiritual practice. Because I continued to face existential and personal challenges, and because I was intellectually curious, I read about other faiths. I began practicing meditation for twenty minutes a day, and I sought out therapy in an attempt to deal with my anxiety and depression.

My life abroad in Europe improved as I found a mentor, a good studio, a gallery dealer, friends, and an art-teaching job. However, I continued to struggle, due in part to the cruelty of a particular family member that created inner havoc, not to mention general, basic self-esteem issues. With hindsight I can see that trauma oiled the engine of my spiritual journey. I had no choice but to dive deep, confident that God's mercy and human spiritual experience were the sole cure.

My textual spiritual journey took me through shamanistic, Buddhist, Hindu, Jewish, and Muslim sacred texts. I was happy to discover that the Qur'an was full of stories found in the two other Abrahamic traditions, from those of Abraham and Moses to those of Mary and Jesus. At the same time, I was discovering and falling in love with the potent visual language of Islamic art and its geometric tessellations mapping the connections of unity, diversity, and infinity.

Although stuck in the mud of existential issues for many years, I was also blessed with visions and extraordinary dreams that provided the hope I needed to keep going. One night, during a most difficult period, I dreamed that I received a letter from a certain 'Monsieur de Nabi.' When I opened it and unfolded the paper, it turned into glowing light, waking me up to a feeling of deep serenity.

I took breakfast and sat on the couch pondering the night vision. "Who is Mr. de Nabi?" I asked myself. Suddenly I remembered the Nabi art movement in France and that *nabi* meant prophet. I intuitively deduced that the dream was a message from the Prophet Muhammad. It was an answer to my prayers, and one to which I should pay heed. I looked up mosques in the phonebook and, only three days later, I found myself taking my *shahadah* in a local mosque. Simply saying "I bear witness that there is no God but God and that Muhammad is his Prophet"—as were the other prophets, including Jesus—makes one a Muslim. This step constituted an overarching healing step for me that allowed me to gain confidence; I felt a universal, sustaining spiritual force begin to cleanse my heart and unite inner and outer life. I found strength to do things that I could not have done before: graduate school and public-speaking, getting married, and simply feeling existential contentment. This does not mean that the path has been all rosy—self-purification is a lifelong task—but the prayer-punctuated days and the beauty of Qur'anic recitation gave me new energy to make good decisions without much effort. It created a clear before and after, albeit one that many did not want to see or hear about.

As long as my Islam remained invisible, I remained within the sphere of white privilege, even if my views were often countered. Months later, when I decided to don the hijab full time, everything changed. I was sometimes refused work and apartments; I was threatened several times, including being almost run over by a car, and I was also treated unfairly by my academic institution despite being a straight-A student. It seemed unbelievably strange that a journey that led me to what I personally needed to heal was now construed as my becoming an ideologically-driven enemy. In short, a new dissociative gap opened between how I felt and how others saw me, reminiscent of the gap that a dysfunctional relative had already gotten me used to. The psychological effect of such cognitive dissonance has been best expressed by W.B. Yeats in his "Dialogue of Self and Soul":

> The finished man among his enemies? –
> How in the name of Heaven can he escape
> That defiling and disfigured shape
> The mirror of malicious eyes
> Casts upon his eyes until at last
> He thinks that shape must be his shape?

Becoming a minority differs from empathising with the minoritized, although my name, skin colour, culture and language can still be considered tools of privilege to a certain degree. All of my academic work to date has been an attempt to build bridges by deconstructing western stereotypes of Islam, particularly visibly-Muslim women, to make space for the self-identities and subjectivities of the 'otherized' to emerge. As a visibly Muslim woman, the only jobs I have found after my Ph.D. have been outside of my native country, in Muslim-majority countries. And so, once again, I am a global nomad, something I would enjoy even more fully if it were out of pure desire.

What led me to envision this volume was the growing normalization of Islamophobia and the witnessing and testimonies of North American and European friends who have been targets of anti-Islam hate crimes or daily discrimination. Recognizing that firsthand story-telling is a kind of social discourse that can forge true interpersonal relationship and impart lived knowledge, and acknowledging that it only takes a couple of people to ruin a great dinner party cum society, my aim here is to abet peace and understanding and to enrich co-existence. I am confident that making the voices and creativity of those who are usually spoken for visible and heard will evince how the universal path of life and creativity unites all travelers without exception.

— *Valerie Behiery,*
Riyadh, Saudi Arabia, 2020

PART ONE:
SHOUTOUT

HOW I FOUND LOVE FROM MY HOMELESS NEIGHBORS
MAHIN IBRAHIM

I had been doing it for years—walking past homeless people like they were decor on a dirty street, occasionally donating a few dollars or leftovers. I've volunteered to help the homeless before, is how I'd rationalize it. Or I'd wonder, what if they use the money for drugs? Los Angeles has the largest homeless population in the U.S. (nearly 60,000), and it was after I moved downtown, close to Skid Row where 5,000 homeless people sleep every night, that I realized I couldn't just ignore the homeless any longer. They were now my neighbors. And like any neighbors, I should get to know them.

I decided to volunteer for Homeless Care Days, a bi-weekly resource fair organized by the city, held at a park. It's a fair where the homeless can get HIV tested, apply for housing, and more. When I asked the coordinator what I'd be doing, he said, "Just show up." So I did. The first time I arrived, the park was mostly empty and the fair was sparse. Jessica, our coordinator, said, "The park rangers came and told the homeless they had to clear out of here with their tents for an EDM concert."

"They can do that?" I asked, horrified.

She nodded.

The next time I went was an overcast day, my favorite in L.A. Though I'd passed the park hundreds of times, I had never visited. The park had a huge lake in the middle with a tall, spurting fountain and flocks of ducks. Moms walked around the block with their babies in strollers. Spanish music blared through a speaker across the street. That day, the park was filled with homeless people, reading and chatting with friends. Jessica put us to work.

We canvassed around the park, handing out fliers about the fair. Prior to this, we read a training manual, which told us to be cautious when speaking with our clients in case they were on drugs or we sensed danger. This wasn't an exaggeration; Jessica said they had shut down the fair for a few months after a violent incident.

I walked around the park with two regular volunteers, Meredith and Stacy. We approached the first group of people who were sitting on a bench, having a chat. I greeted a man on the left, with silver-grey hair and a crew cut. He had a giant purple scar running down his neck which I tried not to look at.

Before I could tell him about the fair, he said, "Please forgive Americans and us. I am sorry for everything we've done."

As a Muslim hijabi, I knew exactly what he was saying. Please forgive us for the anti-Muslim incidents that rose by 65% in one year, resulting in hijabis being murdered on the streets. Please forgive us for having a president who is relentless about pushing through his Muslim travel ban and is quick to tweet Islamophobic remarks.

His words made me feel incredibly loved. I told him there are good people here and he had no need to apologize.

I couldn't stop thinking about him while we walked. Here I was, ready to make social niceties, while this man had cut straight to the truth. I wasn't used to people being so blunt. In our everyday life, we try to be so politically correct, we often say nothing at all. Yet this man was completely unfiltered, offering up love like he was my best friend. As a homeless person, he was... –less. Less guarded, less removed, less indifferent.

As we closed our loop around the park, I saw a homeless woman with a jagged pixie cut, perched on the fence, water bottles at her feet. She had a nervous energy to her, like she couldn't sit still.

"Are you Muslim?" she asked me.

"Yes," I replied.

"Good. I too am a woman of faith." She pointed a finger up at the sky. She then reached out to hug me, and I hugged her back.

Meredith the volunteer admonished me, "You shouldn't have done that."

"She reached out to me, so I reached out to her," I said. How could I do anything else? Here was another instance where people I'd ignored were not only aware of me, but had my back.

Recently at the library, a homeless man asked what I was reading. I showed him *The Road to Mecca* by Muhammad Asad.

"You're Muslim?" he asked.

I nodded.

"That's great!" he exclaimed, as if I had cured a terminal illness.

In America, you're welcomed and loved if you're rich, pretty or famous, not religious. My interactions with these people showed me otherwise. While walking home that day, I was humbled to realize: of all the communities I had encountered, it was the homeless, the most marginalized, who were the most welcoming of all.

YOU'RE INFECTED WITH ISLAMOPHOBIA
AQUIL VIRANI

Ignorance is a sickness.
Insidious.
Contagious.
It's in the water.
A public health issue.
If your parents have it, you probably have it too.
You may have it and not even know.
You can be treated, but only if you want to be treated.
A proper dose of education.
300 mg pills of critical awareness.
Regular exposure to Muslims.
Make sure to get your kids treated too.

SHOUTOUT
SARAH BASHEER

This is a shoutout to the Walmart cashier who said, "I like your tattoos, but I know they're not called that," when I handed her my money with henna clad hands, fresh from Eid.

This is a shoutout to the neon yellow vest wearing cart pusher who stopped my mother and asked if she was Muslim, and when she hesitantly said yes, he said, "Jesus loves you."

This is a shoutout to all the middle-aged men who hold the door open for me, whenever I go shopping.

This is a shoutout to my high school AP Literature teacher who hugged me hello when I was nervous to visit her at school after recently starting to wear my hijab.

This is a shoutout to the older white woman who said I looked beautiful in my heavy and ornate *anarkali* when I stepped out of the hall to go to the restroom at my cousin's wedding.

This is a shoutout to my high school classmates who liked my profile picture after I started wearing hijab.

This is a shoutout to my college stats professor who said my eyeshadow matched my scarf perfectly as she struggled for the right word for my hijab.

This is a shoutout to the woman who tapped my shoulder at a Trump rally, smiled at me and said, "I'm glad you're here."

This is a shoutout to my best friend from sixth grade, Cindy, who after catching up years later, texted me saying, "I'm so proud of you for deciding to wear your hijab. I remember you were nervous about that in high school."

This is a shoutout to my black co-worker from college who came to a Muslim student event, just because I asked him to.

This is a shoutout to the community members who put signs on the doors of my mosque saying, "We love having you in the neighborhood" and "Love trumps hate."

This is a shoutout to every person who stands up for diversity, and a religion and the people who practice it when there's so much hatred. When the media labels Muslims as terrorists. When the Chinese and Israeli and atrocious world governments torture and kill thousands of Muslims. When the American president tries to ban Muslims from entering the country. When white men deface, break into, and set mosques on fire. When Muslim women are harassed, assaulted, and killed in the streets for practicing their faith. When three university students are shot to death in their homes for being Muslims. When it feels like there's no solace for Muslims in the world.

It's because of people who protest at airports, who defend Muslims on the subway, who ally themselves and offer people like me a piece of my humanity back that I can continue walking with my head held high, and continue to love, even in the face of hate.

TALES FROM PUBLIC TRANSPORTATION: EXPERIENCES AND REFLECTIONS TRAVELLING AROUND CHICAGO AS AN AMERICAN MUSLIM • ABDUL-MALIK RYAN

Part I

A conversation while waiting for the bus in a snowstorm at the Harvey Transportation Center:

> Guy A: Are you a lawyer?
>
> Me: I used to be. What makes you ask that?
>
> Guy A: You look like my nephew's lawyer. He's cool.
>
> Guy B: What's that book you're reading about?
>
> Me: Hospitality in Islam.
>
> Guy B: Hospitality in Islam... are you Muslim?
>
> Me: Yeah.
>
> Guy A: You're Muslim? I didn't know you were Muslim. You look like you're Irish or something.
>
> Me: I *am* Irish.
>
> Guy A: I never met an Irish Muslim before.
>
> Me: Well, now you have.

Part II

I can honestly say that in the twenty years since I accepted Islam, I've never for a minute had any doubts I did the right thing. Still, as humans, we all get tired; we all get frustrated. Our tendency, when facing the trials of this world, is to get distracted and discouraged. If we keep our hearts open though, God is always sending us *ayaat* (signs) through his angels and other messengers to refocus us and keep us going.

Nearing my stop, I get up and walk towards the door of the bus to get ready to exit.

Older Gentleman sitting near door (starting to smile): Are you one of those people that you say *salaam* to?

Me: Um, you mean Muslims? Yes, *alhamdulillah*.

27

Gentleman (smiling really wide): Yeah, I thought so. I saw your... (gestures towards my *kufi* and *keffiyeh*. He's giving the most amazing smile now.)

As the door opens and I start to walk out...

Him: *As salaam 'alaykum!*

Me: *Wa 'alaykum as salaam!*

I can't stop smiling the whole walk home.

Part III

Does this ever happen to any of my sisters wearing *abayas*?

I'm walking through the Jackson red line station in my *thobe* (long robe-like garment), and this friendly young kid gives me a big smile and says something to me. I can't hear him exactly so I walk closer, thinking he is saying, *"Salaam 'alaykum,"* which is not uncommon, even from some non-Muslims (especially from Black Americans). However, as I get close, he says to me, "Congratulations! You graduated?"

Jumu'ah Mubarak! (Have a blessed Friday!)

Part IV

Many nights, when school is in session, I find myself coming home pretty late on Metra. Usually that means I'm pretty tired by the time I get to the train station, and sometimes I'll have some time to wait for the next train. When I do, I usually choose to use that time to make the *Isha* (night) prayers, as I will have more concentration than if I wait until I get home, when I'll be even more tired. Also, when you are really tired, it's a great feeling to know that you've gotten all your prayers in, so that if you get home and just lie on the couch or crawl into bed, that's fine. As someone who loves being very identifiable as a Muslim and has been that way for a long time, I often don't think too much about how others perceive me, and I've never been hesitant about praying in public. (I know people of many traditions have mixed feelings about public expressions of religiosity, usually due to questions of intentions. While the Islamic tradition places a high importance on working on one's intentions, there is an undeniable place for public worship in our tradition.)

Last night, as I completed my prayers, a young woman came up to me and seemed very emotional. She shared with me that she could tell I was Muslim, said "*Salaam alaykum*" to me, and said she admired that I was faithful to my religion even in public, even though I might have to endure people looking at me strangely or thinking things about me. I was moved by her comments, mainly because, as I said, she seemed to be very emotional, on the brink of tears, although I didn't know why. I soon found out what must have been a big part of it. As I continued to walk towards my train, the man working at the info desk told me that three different people had come up to him and pointed me out, praying, and asked him if they should call Metra Police. The guy was cool, though. He told them, "What, because he's praying? He does that almost every night." He told me that, recently, there were some Muslim women just sitting in a group, and someone 'reported' them to him, and when he was, like, "Um, they're not doing anything," the person said, "Well, you guys always tell us, 'If you see something, say something.'" He told them, "Yeah, that doesn't mean if you see Muslims..."

This is the nature of this world... good and bad are mixing with each other all the time, even within our own selves, and it is natural, if one is paying attention, to be concerned about some of the scary things around us. But there is nothing to worry about, for surely God is on the side of what's good, and if God is on your side, there is truly nothing to worry about after that.

Part V

You never know who Allah will send to lift your mood and get you in the spirit for that special time of year. Today it was the gentleman from across the train station who saw me and was like, "Hey!" So I looked over to him. Then he yelled what sounded like, "Hey! Ramada this weekend!" but I knew just what he meant. Ya Allah, bring us to your month of blessings!

YOU'RE NOT LOOKING ENOUGH
LEENA BARAKAT

On my dad's side, I'm the only grandchild who wears a hijab, and I think there are seventeen of us. On my mom's side, I'm the only one besides her who does. So why do I do it? My mom put it on when she was twenty-seven. I put it on ten years ago, when I was sixteen years old. I was young. It was a decision I made. It took me a while. I was at a point when I really wanted more for myself. I identified the values and character that I wanted to uphold and live for the rest of my life, and I saw the hijab as a form of insurance towards that. The hijab comes with a level of persona—you don't see hijabis at a club, if you know what I mean. Those are the kinds of things I remember thinking at sixteen years old—I can go this way, or I can go that way.

It's transformed significantly since then. I don't wear it for those reasons anymore. Now, it's become more of a political statement as well. I've been told so many times that I'm very approachable. Random people ask me questions that they tell me they wouldn't have been comfortable to ask otherwise. They tell me I'm very easy to talk to, and open, down to earth. I break a lot of stereotypes in their mind. A hijabi's not supposed to be running a marathon. A hijabi's not supposed to be an outspoken, proud, independent feminist. Hijab and feminism doesn't sound right in the same sentence to so many people. But I remind them why it does. Especially in the 9/11 era, I found it necessary, my way of contributing in a small way.

My cousins are like—why? I'm constantly asked by my own grandfather—when are you going to take it off? I don't feel like I need it the way I used to, but I'm very proud of it. Imagine, from sixteen to now twenty-six. Those are the formative years in so many ways. So it's become a big part of my identity.

It's not just doing it for those Americans who are unaware; it's also like speaking to my own community, the Arabs, saying—you don't have to walk with your head down. As a hijabi, you don't have to wear gloomy colors. Just be... you. If you're wearing it for the right reasons, if you're wearing it because you truly want to wear it, then let your personality come through it. That's something that's always been important for me as a Muslim woman.

I can't tell you how many people have told me—you actually seem very happy! And I'm like—yes, what are you getting at? I don't look like I'm supposed to look in their minds.

When I met my husband, he was staunchly against the hijab. I was like—I'm not going to settle for someone who won't accept it. I need someone who is going to really understand and love it the way that I do, and I totally understand if you want to walk away. I actually made that ultimatum. He was like—you're really sure about it. I had to break his stereotypes. I had to break his image. I was shocked that, for someone who's so educated, so politically conscious, so proud of his Arab roots, he had zero understanding about the hijab. He thought it was an oppressive thing. I broke his barriers and his stereotypes. By now, when I talk about possibly taking it off in the future, he's just surprised, and he's like—I've really grown to love you with it, but whatever you want to do, I'm proud of you. It's been interesting seeing him progress, and in a way that I never pushed. It's a big part of who I am, and I saw him come to love it. So he's supportive either way.

I'm really no different from many other Muslim women. I didn't just become this way by myself out of nowhere. I have a community of very like-minded women, feminists, individuals, who wear the hijab. I'm really no different from them. My husband had never seen anyone like that before, and most people haven't. I feel like sometimes I'm just here to say—you're not looking, you're not looking enough.

It's not for everyone. And I'm so saddened by those women who have to put it on, not because they want to, but because their fathers or some male dominating force in their life is telling them to. You hear those stories, and they're scary. It's definitely something that needs attention and needs to be addressed, but it's just not everyone's story. That's a new idea for some people. And it's like—really, people? It's hilarious, the images they come with in their minds. So many people are like—wow, Leena, your English is very good. Or—when did you come? Fool, I was born in LA. Stop.

* Excerpted and edited from an interview of Leena Barakat by Najib Joe Hakim (from the "Home Away from Home: Little Palestine by the Bay" Project, 2015).

NOTRE SANG, LA MÊME COULEUR II
(OUR BLOOD, THE SAME COLOR)
COMPILED BY AQUIL VIRANI

A large-scale painting full of multilingual messages hangs at the Centre Culturel Islamique de Québec (CCIQ). Words of hope, healing and solidarity adorn the collaborative artwork, created at the Montreal Vigil for Quebec City Muslims outside Parc metro station on Monday, January 30, 2017, the day after a mass shooting at the Quebec City mosque. Those expressions compose this communal poem as compiled by Aquil Virani, the artist of the participatory work.

Defeat hate with love.
Only love ! הבהא קר
All we need is love.

United we are Stronger.
They will not divide us.
No one divides us.

Vous êtes mort dans les bras de Dieu.
We belong to God and to Him we shall return.
Welcome home.

Allah is great. بﻛأ ﻞﻟا Never forget that.
See what happen today?
Is a proof of Hope. Still existing.

Je ne veux pas que nos enfants
grandissent dans la peur.
Don't be afraid of who you are.

Coexist. *L'union fait la force.*
We support you.
We're here for you.

Nous faisons tous partie de grande famille de l'Humanité.
Recognize all humans as one.
One love.

Désolé. We stand with you in your grief.
"And whoever kills one human,
 it's as if they have killed all of humanity."

Allah ya rahmann. Islam pour tout jours.
On apprécie beaucoup le soutien des non musulmans.
May Allah Bless You and your children. You are our home.

We are with you, Québec, *terre d'ouverture.*
Un Québec libre est un Québec uni.
You are home.

We stand on guard with you.
Resistance contre la violence.
Non au racisme. No al racismo.

Solidarity with you and people of all faiths.
Muslims and Jews refusing to be enemies.
La terre est à tout le monde.

No borders. *Nos larmes ont le meme gout,*
notre sang, la même couleur.
Paix. Peace. Shalom. Salaam. سلام

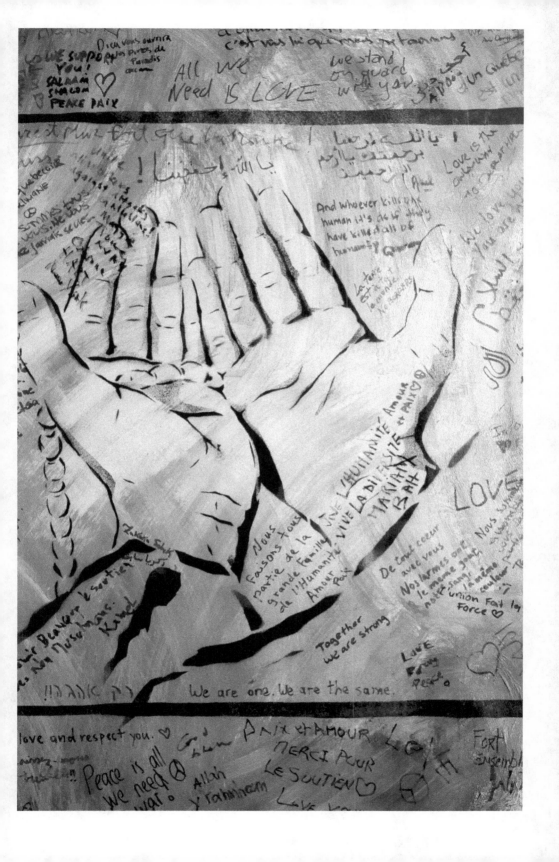

PART TWO: FINDING HOME

ON WHAT IT MEANS TO BE SOMELICAN
SAID FARAH

1. Randy Moss taught me how to run a skinny post.

Bismillah.

I was stripped of my ability to breathe the day I stepped foot into this country. I could feel the power seeping from my pores as I walked through JFK airport after getting off the plane. It'd been twenty-eight hours since the Kenyan Airways 737 took off from Nairobi, and I was four years removed from the last time I'd been in America. As a Black Muslim man in post-9/11 America, I knew that I would be targeted for questioning by Homeland Security. As someone who was born in Somalia, I knew that my country's political history, especially in relation to the U.S., made me an automatic suspect. I'd heard of the dozens of young Somali men who'd made their way back home and joined extremely violent organizations. I knew that these young men looked, talked and dressed just like me, were raised in the U.S. just like me, and had grown disillusioned with life as a third-class citizen just like me. Unlike me, they'd been convinced that going back to a country they had no ties with was a noble cause worth dying for. Unlike them, I only went back to Somalia to find pieces of myself that I'd lost on the road to American assimilation.

When I was in Africa, I used to imagine how my conversations sounded to the NSA tech listening to them in his booth the next day. It is a peculiar feeling to know that you are being surveilled, so much so that you cannot speak on the phone without using measured language that will decrease the likelihood of you being flagged by some secret department of the government.

I knew that there was nothing I could do to avoid my fate other than to practice patience. I've been to the psych ward before, many times in fact. While there, I realized the futility of proving your sanity to people who've already written you off as hopelessly crazed. It is the same futility as that of a Black man accused of rape by a white woman in the Deep South, sitting in his jail cell and waiting for the sheriff to hand him over to the lynch mob outside. Futility.

It is futility which informs my decision-making process in airports. Futility tells me to be on guard at all times, look straight ahead, and walk with a measured gait. It forces me to be extra-conscious of my body and its relation to the cameras recording my every move. Futility allows me to see through the eyes of whoever is watching the screen recording me, and those eyes tell me to avoid unnecessary conversations with strangers, to act normal, but not too normal. Futility is what I call being stared down by the nine-dollar-an-hour TSA agent who sits in rush hour traffic listening to Rush Limbaugh wax bombastic about the impending Muslim invasion, about a "Creeping Sharia" which threatens to overtake this nation's "conservative family values." It is almost always this kind of agent who singles me out for extra screening. It is almost always someone who is ignorant of his own past, of the fact that Thomas Jefferson kept a copy of the Qur'an in his library, that he used it as a framework for understanding the future of this nation, and that it helped inform his decisions in co-drafting a more inclusive constitution that would stand the test of time. Never mind that he owned slaves. Knowing all this, it should not have come as a surprise to me when the agent asked to swab my hands a second time with the cotton cloth used to collect explosive residue for testing in an Ion-Mobility Spectrometer. I tried to speak in a confident tone when I replied that I'd already passed that test. He must not have believed the results because, with a pained expression and bored tone, he said, "I know. Please stick your palms out again."

This American life is an injustice in motion. The most common phrase used to frame people like me is our "potential for radicalization." The most radical thing I've ever done is skateboard down the hills of Seattle at midnight as the rain fell in sideways sheets; I couldn't be more American. Truthfully, defending my right to exist is a trying experience. I'm forced to be a model citizen for so many categories that it makes my head spin. Yes, I'm Black, but I'm not dangerous. Yes, I'm Somali, but I'm not dangerous. Yes, I'm Muslim, but I'm not dangerous. Yes, I'm a writer, but – wait. The act of bending language carries its own sense of purpose, to reclaim power stolen from us by those who subjugate, so maybe writing *is* a dangerous act.

What I'm trying to say is that I wasn't surprised when they picked me for a "random" screening at the airport that day and every other day like it. I was waiting for it to happen. In Islam we call that acceptance. My therapist would call it anxiety. I know I'm not guilty, but that doesn't prevent me from feeling guilty because of the way others treat me. Have treated me. Will continue to treat me. But God's plan is mysterious, and it's not my place to question it. As Muslims, we believe that real power lies in accepting one's fate and being able to give thanks just the same. Alhamdulillah.

"Excuse me, sir," I heard from behind me, just as I thought I'd made it through customs.

I was relieved when I turned around and saw a Black face in a TSA uniform. He may be an agent of the state, I thought, but at least he's Black. He must've been nervous, though, because as soon as I finished my turn-around and made eye contact, his phone flew out of his hands. It twisted and turned through the air, finally landing with a loud smack. It clattered and skidded across the tiled floor and stopped at my feet. On the screen was an enlarged picture of me from my passport. There was a big red X on the top right of the screen. I didn't have to guess what that X meant – selected for questioning. On the flight over, I'd tried to think of every possible defense for being gone from the country for so long, and in a part of the world that was known for extremely violent activities. I had to play defense, even though I had nothing to defend. This is what Islamophobia does to you.

"Why were you in Somalia, sir?"
Because I needed to reconnect with my culture.
"Who were you with?"
My family.
"Do you hate America?"
Hate is a strong word. There's good and bad to be found in
     every place.

"Are you a terrorist?"
The only thing I terrorize is a plate of rice and goat meat
        after a long run.

All the money in the world couldn't have saved me that
interrogation. My parents had always told me to just cooperate and
answer their questions. A friend of mine, also Somali, makes it a point
to give those guys a hard time if they stop him. When I asked him why
he did that, he replied, "Because they're banking on us being meek and
compliant and scared. That's how they exercise power over us. But if
we stand up to their unfair questioning, if we act like the citizens we
are, eventually they'll get tired of harassing us. I'll harass them back
until that day."

2. "It's the tyranny of the American dream that scares me." – Bharati Mukherjee

One American thing I've struggled with is the concept of
forced gratitude. Gratitude is held over our heads, as the perpetual
Others that we are, and we're held under a microscope. If you aren't
grateful enough, the thinking goes, then maybe you don't deserve to
be in this country. Why do I have to be grateful to you, America? Can
I not critique your hypocrisy? Would it not make me *more* of a citizen,
not less, when I shined a light on your glaring deficiencies?
        The only way to describe my assimilation experience in this
country is to say that I was co-opted by America. Coming to America
at age seven, I already had a worldview that clashed with Americanism.
My native culture conflicted too much with this culture's ideas of what
I should be, so something had to give. To make room for America, I
had to rid myself of my Somali-ness, and in so doing, I lost everything
I knew to be true of myself. I washed my identity away to facilitate
integration. I learned to speak English with no accent because, as my
parents repeated ad nauseum, an accent would relegate me to a life of

menial labor. This resonated with me. I worked harder than any child that age should have to.

I grew more isolated by the day as I strived to make America accept me. Because of my concerted use of language, my classmates called me an Oreo – Black on the outside, white on the inside. But how could I tell them that I didn't know what it meant to be Black until I came to America – because in Africa, everyone is Black, and none of them are viewed negatively because of it. As I learned more English, my grasp of the Somali language began to fade. My cultural understanding regressed so quickly that by the time I showed up at family events as a pre-teen, I was told that I wasn't considered Somali; Ciyaal Maraykan – American Kid. They said that, if anything, I was more African American[1] than I was Somali. So there I was: not a real Somali and not a real Black because Black America had already told me that I wasn't Black enough for them. I was Black, but I wasn't *Black-Black*. I didn't walk with a bop or wear Starter jackets. I was an African Booty Scratcher, a Feed The Children infomercial.

All these incidents of casual Othering caused my reality to slip like tectonic plates rubbing against one another. I felt that no matter how hard I tried in school, my teachers' expectations of me were set lower and lower each year. I was slowly being forced to recognize the color of my skin; it had a power all its own, a power which I couldn't deny. A power which limited me. I didn't realize it at the time, but I was

1 Side note: There is a lot of ingrained hate of blackness in my culture. Most Somali people think of themselves as "dark Arabs," not Africans, which is a wild concept to wrap your head around; how does someone born in Africa not qualify as African? I'd like to think it's a remnant of colonization, but something in me wants to say that we've had this issue for longer than that. Somali people are naturally arrogant and love placing themselves in an arbitrary hierarchy, which happens to fall in line with Eurocentric beauty standards. There is also a dark history of slavery in Somalia that is rarely discussed. In fact, the very idea of what it means to be Somali is highly contested and falls along lines of physical traits that were used as justification for enslaving other Africans who were deemed inferior because they were "not Somali." This undiscussed heritage plays itself out today in a multi-tiered caste structure back home, with Somali Bantus still denied access to that elusive "Somali-ness" and treated like second-class citizens.

fighting hundreds of years of conscious and subconscious bias against people who looked like me, a firm belief that Black people didn't belong in places of learning, in professional jobs, or even in possession of life.

I was bumping into a glass ceiling that I wasn't aware of until it smacked me upside the head. By the time I hit middle school, I'd made up my mind to become a neurosurgeon because it was the smartest sounding thing I knew of. It came as a great shock when I was met with ridicule for daring to dream so highly above my station, while my white classmates were encouraged no matter how unrealistic their dreams were in comparison to mine. It reminds me of a passage from Richard Wright's *Black Boy:*

> "What grade are you in school?"
> "Seventh, ma'am."
> "Then why are you going to school?" she asked in surprise.
> "Well, I want to be a writer," I mumbled, unsure of myself;
> > I had not planned to tell her that, but she had made
> > me feel so utterly wrong of no account that I needed
> > to bolster myself.
> "A what?" she demanded.
> "A writer," I mumbled.
> "For what?"
> "To write stories," I mumbled defensively.
> "You'll never be a writer," she said. "Who on earth put such
> > ideas into your nigger head?"
> "Nobody," I said.
> "I didn't think anybody ever would," she declared indignantly.
> As I walked around her house to the street, I knew that
> > I would not go back. The woman had assaulted my
> > ego; she had assumed that she knew my place in life,
> > what I felt, what I ought to be, and I resented it
> > with all my heart. Perhaps she was right; perhaps I
> > would never be a writer; but I did not want her to
> > say so.

3. "You did not leave home like this. This is what the journey does."

– Maaza Mengiste

I'm an outsider, a transient, existing in spaces you can't imagine. I live within your inability to conceptualize my being. You and I are the same – different myths that shape a singular interpretation of infinite ways of being. A shame, what a damn shame. But shame is a choice. To be shamed is to be Somali. Can I live without judgement, Adeer Macaan[2]? Sometimes I wish there were a self-help book for people like us – born in one place, raised in another, belonging to neither. If that book existed, I might find the peace to be myself without fear of prying eyes stabbing me with ill intent. If I could talk to those eyes, I would say: please remember that hurting others won't ease your hurt.

To fight the shame-machine, my fellow Somalis, we must learn to be kind to ourselves. Do we go to mosque to pray, or to be seen praying; to avoid being shamed for not being seen praying? Faith lies within, Adeer Macaan, so how do you know what I believe based on how I talk? Why do you care how long my hair is? And if we're talking about each other's faults, Adeer Macaan, let me ask you this:

B

L A

N K

I'm not going to air out your dirty laundry because part of being a good Muslim is concealing the faults of your fellow Muslim.

---

2 *Adeer Macaan:* Literally, Sweet Uncle. An honorific used to denote respect for an elder, though they don't need to be your actual uncle to deserve the title. In a culture based on the balance between honor and shame, it is important to lead with respect. To be disrespectful, either willingly or erringly, is to bring shame onto not only yourself but also your entire family, your clan, your community. Shame is the currency of political progression in our culture. One uses this term for someone who is owed respect, even if that person is actively disrespecting you. Two shames do not an honor make; someone must maintain their composure.

4. Some days are easy, others like running on broken ankles. Blue eyes, blonde hair; why do you stare?

There's this weird thing I noticed this morning. I am crippled by… what? In my culture, the youth are reprimanded for speaking up. We are expected to keep our mouths shut, especially if an elder is in the room. This gives elders free leeway to do what they will, acting egregiously, with no reprimand. No one is checking the elders. No one is speaking their mind, other than those who are in power. You are slashed down by samurai swords if you dare speak up[3].

At the same time, the youth realize that it's a fundamental tenet of Islam to respect your elders and to maintain family ties. So, even if your loved one is in error, it's incumbent on you as a Muslim to be patient with them. It's said that the way you treat your parents is how your children will treat you. So I keep quiet, to the best of my ability, and hope for Allah's Mercy.

To be who I am in America is a tall order. Everyone who looks at me sees something different. Almost always, it is fear which underlies their impressions of me. I feel this fear but still glide to the next stage in life. My friend wears a hijab. She is very rigidly placed within her societal role. People see her and understand her to be one-dimensional, a placeholder for what they need her to be, based on popular narratives. When they look at me, all they see is a shifting, kaleidoscopic, Rorschach blob on blotter paper. Will I rob them? Will I pray for them? Will I steal their wives? Will I get the same job we both applied for because of quote/unquote affirmative action (lol, no)? Will I be able to speak the same language as them? When did I get here? What was it like back home? Where did I learn to climb trees like that (are you calling me a monkey?)?

---

3 You, I, We. They're all interchangeable in Somali. This is the hard part about reading an English writer whose first language is not this. I flip my persons like wrestlers on a mat. I might include a preface to my writing: "Warning: the author may switch his voices, persons and tenses back and forth as his shifting understanding of reality deems fit. The author is not a linguist. The author is a writer. He uses words; he doesn't decipher them."

Racism is an extrinsic process. Everything about it is explicitly implied – the bulge of the eyes, the width of the smile. Fetishization, commodification. I am a product to you, am I not? I must be, because you don't talk *to* me. You talk *at* me like one would talk at a victim of the Human Zoos[4] of the 19th and 20th centuries. I'm talking about entire villages of Black people displayed naked in cages. I'm talking about a progressive Seattle past which doesn't mention a franchise called the Coon Chicken Inn. To enter this place, you had to walk through the mouth of a twelve-foot-high coon caricature. Inside, you could find knives, matchboxes, coasters, and napkins emblazoned with ever-more-racist depictions of black people. The walls were covered with porters and pink-lipped black faces, smiling with teeth missing, smiles wider than the sea; taller than the mass of bones at the bottom of the Atlantic, bones of middle passage. A smile which isn't a smile. A grimace caused by the dancing flames licking at the corners of a Black man's mouth, peeling back his skin, melting the subcutaneous fat below his lips and exposing his teeth before his body was burnt to a smoldering crisp on the same branch that he was lynched from. Skin melts, you know, if you heat it high enough. Just a few years ago, you wanted to hang and melt me; now you tell me that race is not an issue. Interesting. Take me to the Coon Chicken Inn and we'll revisit that conversation.

4 From the Ferris State University, Jim Crow Museum of Racist Memorabilia: "Human Zoos… [or] ethnographic zoos were often predicated on unilinealism, scientific racism, and a version of Social Darwinism. A number of them placed indigenous people (particularly Africans) in a continuum somewhere between the great apes and human beings of European descent… Scholars argue that human zoos can be linked to three distinct but interrelated phenomena: the construction of an imaginary Other; the theorization of a 'hierarchy of races'; and the construction of colonial empires. The historian Pascal Blanchard and coauthors write that: 'Human zoos, the incredible symbols of the colonial period and the transition from the nineteenth to twentieth century, have been completely suppressed in our collective history and memory. Yet they were major social events. The French, Europeans and Americans came in their tens of millions to discover the "savage" for the first time in zoos or "ethnographic" and colonial fairs. These exhibitions of the exotic (the future "native") laid the foundations on which, over an almost sixty-year period, was spun the West's progressive transition from a "scientific" racism to a colonial and "mass" racism affecting millions of "visitors" from Paris to Hamburg, London to New York, Moscow to Barcelona.'"

Also from the Jim Crow Museum: "All of the objects in the Jim Crow Museum have market values. In 2011, there were more than 50,000 collectors of 'Black Americana', a category that includes racist artifacts. Generally, the more racist an object is, the higher the price it commands."

HIRAETH: FINDING HOME
SHABNAM MAHMOOD

I was aimlessly perusing my Facebook feed when I came across a word I'd seen multiple times before in other posts. I typically pause each time I see this word, reflect, and then keep scrolling. This time it felt different. This time the Welsh word, *hiraeth,* which means homesickness for a home to which you cannot return, or for a home which may have never been, tugged at something inside of me.

Home.

Home.

Home.

I roll the word around in my mind conjuring up so many images. None of the images have anything to do with the current view from my window, a window that is relatively new, for my family and me at least. We've only just moved here. In all honesty, this home should be a dream come true; however, it stems from a nightmare.

It's been a few years since my father passed away. I wish I could say it was a type of death that was poetic or venerated, but there is nothing audacious about dying from stage four cancer, at least not in my father's case. It was a long, arduous ordeal for both my father and our family. My father was brave when it came to his family, not so much so when it came to his health. A sort of feigned bravado justified missed appointments and tests. My father was a very proud man, yet a very stubborn man. It was challenging for him to swallow the bitter truth that the consequences of his health were his alone.

My husband and I have been professional health advocates for my parents, always in touch with doctors, therapists, hospitals, juggling appointments, meetings and such. Despite desperate requests, threats, pleadings, negotiations, my father did not feel the need to keep his appointments—that is until his health worsened. The appointment that changed the course of all of our lives is clear-cut in my mind today. My father and husband walked into the apartment, my father's face dark although he attempted to smile. My husband broke the news to my mother and me. My guts felt like they had fallen to the floor. I was desperately trying to match this new narrative to the man standing before me. How could this be? Why him? Why now? Why?

My brother, who never had a particular inclination towards familial responsibilities, was not home at the time. My mother would leave the responsibility of filling him in to me. This was typical in our family. My mother comes from a long line of male scion enablers. In our culture, as I guess in many others, the sons were favored while the daughters were brought up to look after the fathers and sons. Perhaps they thought this was a sort of practice for marriage.

Nonetheless, growing up, my brother had every freedom imaginable with none of the responsibility. My father was stereotypical in that he attempted to be more firm with my brother, but that didn't come without my mother smothering him with devotion to compensate. Eventually, my father's love for my mother gave way to my brother getting his way. I would do anything for my father who would do anything for my mother who did everything for my brother. I felt like a prayer bead on a vicious thread, repeatedly following a pattern in hopes of a different outcome each time.

I looked around my parents' apartment, trying to find something to latch on to, to keep myself from falling physically and emotionally. I glanced at my mother. My husband told us the doctor's prognosis: my father was expected to live four to twelve years. As I tried to find my guts and some semblance of reality, as it were, I had to face the fact that I now may have only four to twelve years with my father. He was supposed to live longer than that. He was in his early sixties. My father was supposed to see my children grow up, graduate, get married. Now suddenly there was an expiry date on him? The thread of my prayer beads was weakening. It was threatening to break and spill the beads all over.

I lived in the apartment above my parents on Chicago's north side. Prior to that, my husband and I had lived with my parents until the time our twins had announced their arrival. Miraculously, the apartment above us vacated, and my husband and I decided to move upstairs, exactly ten steps, to stay close to my parents while still maintaining our independence. My mother was only too eager to bid me farewell. My father would mosey on upstairs while the furniture delivery happened, then go downstairs to report to my mother: "The furniture is very nice." My husband put up our curtains, arranged the living room furniture, and decorated our home according to how I wanted it. I couldn't get used to it. I would escape to the bathroom to cry my eyes out. My whole life my mother kept me under her thumb lovingly. I wasn't allowed out of her sight. Now suddenly since I got married, she very easily cast me aside since I "had someone to look after" me. I'd been an afterthought for my mother. Her world revolved around only one sun, her son. I was the apple of my father's eye, and that was my saving grace. My father was my rock. He accompanied me to doctor's appointments, school visits; everywhere I expected my mother, my father was only too happy to fill in. He wiped my tears after my first heartbreak, pressed my feet after my first shift of work, and heard every sordid detail of a failed friendship. I couldn't understand why my mother was so willing to let me go. I was used to a lifetime of serfage. I couldn't get used to this freedom. Something told me I would, in time. I would not only get used to this freedom; I would covet it, protect it with every ounce of my being.

My parents' apartment was on the second floor, as the first floor was a row of businesses in the building. My parents' only second floor neighbor was Maria, a single mother who worked her fingers to the bone to make a life for her daughter and herself. She would leave her apartment keys with us whenever she visited Mexico. We would give her bags and bags of clothes to give to the needy there. We would clean her immaculate apartment, water her plants, check her mail and fill her fridge with food when she returned; she brought back gifts for us. For years we were a family.

My upstairs neighbor was Carmen. We had a similar routine of looking out for one another. Every Eid and birthday our children would be spoiled by these two Latinas who did not see us as the Muslims portrayed in the media but as family. With no other family to speak of here in the United States, this was a comfort to me.

We came to this country as refugees when Idi Amin expelled all Asians from Uganda in 1972. Generations of families living under one roof for years were now scattered across the globe. Amin did not see us as Ugandans. He saw us as leeches that came and took advantage of 'their' economy. He accused Asians of not integrating with Ugandans. I have aunts, uncles, and cousins to prove otherwise. One side of my family came to Uganda in the late 1800s, brought by the British to build railroads. When offered a chance to stay, they did, flourishing in trade. The other half of my family was in the British Army, and after WWII they chose to settle in Uganda, given India's distressed economic state at the time. Some were initially brought by British Asians; others came to Uganda of their own accord to make a better life. Both were part of the economic backbone of the country, reaching into the various echelons of government and commerce.

I was barely a year old when we left Uganda, and after a stint at a refugee camp in Rome, my family was on a plane to New York, soon to settle in Lancaster, Pennsylvania. The story goes—as my parents related it to me numerous times—we were picked up at the airport in Harrisburg and taken to a home in Lancaster on Atkins Avenue. My mother spoke almost no English. She held on to my brother, who was six at time, and me. Our sponsors showed us around the house and said they would return the next day. My parents believed we would be taken to a refugee camp eventually, as was the case with other Asian refugees. The house had three bedrooms and one bath. Every type of convenience was available, from food in the fridge to a thread and needle. My parents spent the night with my brother and me on the sofa so as not to disturb anything in whosever's house this was. The following morning the sponsors came to check on us and were shocked when they found out we slept in the living room. They assumed we knew it was our house.

It took a month for my parents to convey to the sponsors that we needed Asian groceries. So it was off to New York and the Asian markets, which were only a few shops at that time, but it brought overwhelming emotion to my mother when she saw our familiar comestibles: dals, spices, grains, as well as kitchenware staples like a patlo, which is a round wooden board to roll chapatis on; a velan rolling pin, and a sev machine, an instrument used to make a savory snack. Once back at Atkins Avenue, the first meal my mother made with her newfound provisions was kidney bean curry, dal, rice, and chapatis. Although I don't remember any of this, this simple fare in that one moment made the house on Atkins Avenue somewhat of a home. I like to think of it as the refugees' banquet.

When we learned that my father had stage four cancer, I found myself in a familiar situation. I had to break the news to my older brother. I was downstairs at my parents' apartment, sitting at the dining table with my brother and mother staring at me. I approached the topic with straightforwardness: "Dad has stage four cancer." They kept staring. "The doctors have given him four to twelve years." They kept staring. While my mother may have initially heard the news from my husband, it wasn't fully confirmed for her until her son heard it from his sister. I looked around the dining room, letting the news sink in. I thought they might be in shock, and it was best just to let them take the news in at their own pace. When they're ready, I thought, we can discuss it further.

During their silence, I remembered all the events that took place in this very room. The twelve-by-fifteen space had seen my teenage years turn into my twenties, my wedding celebrations, the surprise announcement my husband and I had hung on the cream-colored walls to let my family know they were about to become grandparents and an uncle, the devastation of telling my parents of my miscarriage, family birthdays, Thanksgiving dinners, Eid feasts, family fights, graduation parties, slowly watching myself grow as we awaited with bated breath the arrival of our twins, family meetings, my parents giving their grandchildren baths in their little table-top tub....

My mother and brother began crying. I went back to staring at the ghosts of my memories; they were easier to deal with.

I remember being upstairs sleeping in my bedroom, which was right above my parents' bedroom, when the ambulance siren slowly begin screaming until the sound faded away. Something felt different. My fears were verified when, a half hour later, my mother confirmed my father had to be taken in. And so began the month-long vigil of watching my father die a slow and painful death.

My father's four brothers and three sisters came from overseas to be with him at the end. I wish they hadn't. I wanted these last moments to be, for once, of peace, and it ended up being a circus. Each sibling had a cell phone which was used to boisterously facetime, email, call and text family and friends overseas. One small hospital room with so many visitors tired my father out. Instead of allowing my mother or my family the time with my father, his siblings commandeered his hospital room. We were relegated to the roles of cook and chauffeur. At my father's behest, we didn't say anything. We quietly endured it all. I struggled with all this. My husband and I were my father's advocates. The doctors spoke only to us. This irritated his family to no end. Arguments ensued. We allowed them to discuss whatever they wished with the doctors, but that wasn't enough. They didn't see my father was to spend his last days in a hospital room. He would never see his home again. The doctor came in and said that after a month of trying, it was now best to shift my father to a hospice. He had a week at best.

My father lived on Prince Charles Street in Kampala, Uganda. I grew up hearing stories from my parents about "back home." He relished me with tales of teenage escapades of going on safaris, packing an open-back truck filled with friends and cousins to go to the drive-in, his first job at a print shop. My mother shared stories of her upbringing while we sat at the dining table cleaning cilantro and prepping dinner. Having lived alone, without any family around, I yearned for my parent's memories. I may have been less than a year old when we left Uganda, but I felt as if I had lived all these adventures through my parents. I yearned for Uganda. I yearned for "back home."

"If you only had known what it was like to…." set off a

number of wistful dreams my parents wished for me. Growing up as an Indian girl in a predominantly white neighborhood, I was often asked: "Where are you from?" When I replied, "Uganda," the response was an immediate: "Where's that?" Once they heard East Africa the response was: "But you don't look Black!" Hence, a lifelong struggle of finding my identity. Here I was, an Indian girl from Uganda in Dutch-Amish country. The number of minority students in my school could be counted on one hand. I couldn't look to them to help me understand how to tackle this dilemma of identity. Most of them had assimilated to the WASP doctrine. This left me more confounded than ever about my own identity. I did everything to fit it, spoke flawless English, wore English clothing, cooked English food (I could out-bake any Amish). Yet I couldn't fit in. I recalled my parents' stories of Uganda. I yearned to be there. I wouldn't have to worry about fitting in.

It was the early Eighties. My parents were not conservative Muslims. There was no mosque in Lancaster. The only mosque was eighty-some miles away in Allentown, and it was a Shia mosque. It suited my mother, although we were Sunni. At least it was something. All the Asians there were from Uganda and Tanzania. This added to my confusion. I had endeavored my entire life to emulate the life of Uganda. I taught myself Swahili by speaking to my parents and the community members. What I came to realize is that the dialects of Swahili from Uganda and Tanzania differed greatly. Tanzanian Swahili is like the Queen's English, proper, poetic, distinguished. The choppy Swahili I spoke made me sound undignified, lowly, stupid. I stuck out like a sore thumb in the Shia community. Although we were all from East Africa, we were different. Now, all of a sudden, I didn't want to be like everyone from "back home" Uganda. I desired to be like the upper echelons of Tanzanians with their dialect of Swahili rolling off of the tongue like poetry. I didn't realize the society I was so desperate to be a part of was elitist. Once you're known as an outsider, you can't be accepted. Ironically, I had the best reputation amongst marriage-aged Shia girls in their community. I knew how to cook, clean, and had the best grades. I tutored a lot of the Shia girls. Many 'aunties' from various Shia households contacted my mother with proposals for me, until they found out I was Sunni. If these aunties were confused, they needn't have worried. This was the one time I saw my father defeat my mother's wishes. I was not to marry a Shia.

I was a sickly child, spending much of my childhood in the hospital. Well-meaning aunties at the Shia mosque did what they could to help pray for me. I found myself being tied with a white cloth to a pole with a hand at the top. Everyone was dressed in black. They were chanting prayers and beating their chests. I wondered if they were trying to frighten my illness out of me. Most of their religious practices were ritualistic, something foreign to me. I went along with everything because I didn't want to stick out and wanted to be accepted. My mother welcomed their concern and friendship, but she didn't tell my father what was being done.

Once the Ugandan-Asian Sunnis got around to it, they began organizing a community in Lancaster. The resurgence of Islam which brought about the hijab hadn't taken place yet. Everyone wore their traditional dresses with colorful pins in their hair. There was no Islamic school, no Islamic education. There was only one Pakistani family in Lancaster who volunteered to teach the community kids the Qur'an. A community aunty took me there only once.

Everyone in the community was either an aunt or an uncle. What kind depended on their relationship with one's parents. Mother's sister was masi. Masi's husband was masa. Mother's brother was mama. Mama's wife was mami. Father's sister was fui. Fui's husband was fua. Father's brother was thaiya or chacha, depending on whether they were older or younger than one's father. I took to calling all the women 'fui' and all the men 'mama,' even if they were husband and wife. In my young mind it made sense, though I didn't understand why it amused the community to no end. I was given the task by an uncle to type up the official community telephone book, a sort of telephone tree for the community, filled with names of husbands and wives, addresses and phone numbers. I remember being given material for a *shalwaar kameez* as a thank-you gift. It was a monumental moment for me. To think I did something for the community at the age of sixteen. I looked at my Casio typewriter and felt proud. We never got to enjoy the fruits of our labor as we moved to Chicago soon after.

Chicago brought us out of our small-town mindset to a big-city dilemma. Here we found Indians and Pakistanis galore. Where once when I was little and spotted a saree-clad woman in New York, I would break out in rapture, here I was overwhelmed. Devon Avenue west of Western Avenue was known as "Little India." East of Western and Devon Avenue was known as "Little Pakistan." The one Pakistani family in Lancaster had been very nice. Here no one looked at you. If we were lucky enough to strike up a conversation with Indians, the first question was: "Where are you from?" meaning which part of India do you hail from? It was the same with Pakistanis. As soon as Uganda was mentioned, the interest in their eyes dropped like a brick. "But you speak Urdu!" "But you speak Hindi!" "But you speak Gujarati!"

What they couldn't have known was that the Asian community in Uganda became one homogenous entity. Speaking multiple languages was common. Ugandans shared everything. Language. Food. Festivals. So it came as a shock to us to see the discrimination in Chicago Asians. The narrative I had come to use for non-Asians was now being used for Asians. A simple conversation couldn't be had until it was explained how we could possibly speak multiple languages, not be Black, and maintain our religion and culture. And even after all that, the only response was a frown and a puzzled look. We didn't fit in.

Time heals all wounds. After twenty-plus years in Chicago, we've finally found community and friends. When my father passed away, it was this community that came to our aid and offered comfort. When I was young in Lancaster, I used Ghulam Sarwar's book, *Islam,* to teach myself the fundamentals and learn how to pray. Now my children are going to an Islamic full-time school, and it is through this experience that I came to the decision to wear the hijab and learn more about Islam. Through our involvement in the school we became part of a community, not just Indians and Pakistanis, but Somalis, Bosnians, Arabs, and more. It was my version of Uganda. One homogenous community. What I have come to learn in all my years of a nomadic existence is that every time I felt lost, I looked towards my mother. If her smile reached her eyes when she looked at me, I imagined I would finally find my home.

My brother passed away recently. It was sudden and shocking. The *tasbeeh* broke and the prayer beads were scattered. My seventy-three-year-old mother is bearing the pain with as much patience as she can muster. He was her everything. After his death my mother was alone, so we decided to vacate both apartments, upstairs and downstairs, and move to the suburbs. Maria and Carmen were devastated but understood. This new apartment is large with three bedrooms and two bathrooms, a boon for our family. It provides all the conveniences we need: an elevator for my mother, as she is disabled with arthritis, laundry on two floors, the most engaging neighbors. Despite it all, it cannot assuage my mother's feelings that she's a burden. It's still all new. I'm looking to find that lost thread, to string the beads again. I don't know where we'll go from here, but for now I'm looking at my mother's eyes while she's looking for home elsewhere, where my brother is.

SUNDAY LUNCH IN EXILE
ENESA MAHMIC

We didn't talk about our suffering.
We taught our children patience
Mastering the silent endurance.
Our masters said:
Unnecessary sorrows hijack the glory of God
So we ate the crumbs from their table
Without any complaint.
We comforted ourselves: *I'm fine. It's ok.*
Tomorrow will be the same.
The concept of discrimination repeats itself.
Gentleman from social institution will remind me again
That I'm just a number in the system.
I will be thinking again
How I should leave everything
Maybe move to another city, another country.
I comfort myself with illusions of love,
Understanding and forgetfulness
But deep in my heart I know
There is no country for immigrants.

THE MAN WHO TALKS TO BIRDS
ENESA MAHMIC

Once in Forest Park
I met a foreigner who was feeding the birds
Last sunset of the dying autumn
Mirrored in his eyes.

He told me:
Dear friend,
My English is almost incomprehensible.
I can't talk to people.
I'm just sitting on banch and speaking with birds.

I AM THE MUSLIM
WENDY DIAZ

I am Wendy, the Muslim. I am not much different from you.
I come from three generations that fought for the red, white and blue.
Grew up as an Army brat in a military family,
but you may not guess that just by looking at me.

You see a veil, and though it is over my head,
it is almost as if it's covering your eyes instead.
I am an immigrant, at least that's what you like to call me,
although Puerto Ricans were given U.S. citizenship in 1917.

Settled in Georgia, traveled Alaska and the Northwest,
lived in sunny Arizona, and don't mess with Texas.
Lived in base after base, too many to name.
I am not a Mexican, but to you it's all the same.

I stood with the anthem time after time, hand on my chest,
went to baseball games and learned English without an accent.
I was content with living in the land of the free,
knowing religious choice was part of the guarantee.

You see, I may have never known about Islam
had I stayed back in my original homeland.
So why be surprised I chose this path
when it was this country that gave me the chance?

This was all part of a greater plan,
so when you see me, look closer; there is more to who I am.

I am the Puerto Rican, the Muslim.
I am the Army brat, the Muslim
I am the immigrant, the Muslim.
I am the American, the Muslim.
I am the Muslim.

HOME AGAIN
HANAA WALZER

Where is home? This is a question I've asked myself and others, wherever I've lived. I was born on one continent, raised on another, and married someone from yet another continent. I've felt aspects of home in each, but the question isn't as simple as this. Some aspect of home always eludes me, but I do believe I've stumbled upon an answer that quenches my thirst. As a Muslim, I guess true home, ultimately, can only be found in Jenna (Paradise). Every other place, every other feeling, is only a reminiscence and a reminder of what we should truly be striving for. Nevertheless, respite is promised after each hardship, and safety is yearned for in any unfamiliar setting. But in reality, the truest home is as elusive as lasting happiness. It's a fleeting feeling, a constantly-escaping sense of security and calm, which is likely to be snatched away at any given moment. The memory of the feeling persists, however, and allows for renewed hope to find it again; it motivates our constant search, and grants us a paragon when we think we may have finally found it.

I was born in a place that was not native to either my mother, who was born in the U.S. by her Mi'kmaq parents, or my father, who was born and raised in Zurich by his Swiss parents. My father's paternal ancestors had journeyed from northern India to Hungary in search of religious freedom and safety from persecution, eventually settling in Ticino in Switzerland four centuries ago. My father's father left Ticino for Zurich for work. My father's maternal ancestors were Swiss as far back as Switzerland existed.

My mother's ancestors had journeyed from Canada to Massachusetts, commuting back and forth between the U.S. and another Mi'kmaq reservation, where hundreds of other Mi'kmaq people were relocated through "centralization," a convenient misnomer that forced dozens of families to abandon their homes to make the administrative task of keeping track of their movements easier on government workers. Nomadism is in my blood, though I lived in the same building for sixteen of the first eighteen years of my life.

I was raised in Ticino, the Italian part of Switzerland, which makes up about twelve percent of the Swiss population and was my grandfather's home canton, as it was his own grandfather's. In Switzerland language defines you to a large extent; my father's Zurcher accent, and the fact that we spoke English at home, clearly positioned us outside the standard norm. We didn't mind, as English was a 'cool' language, and although it set us apart, it did so in a positive way. Growing up I was, therefore, acutely aware of what it meant to speak the 'right' languages, and the 'wrong' ones. Language is clearly a very useful tool if you know how and when to use it, but it could just as easily be turned against you. I became adept at switching codes when needed, and was able to disguise my accents and pick up on all sorts of subtleties that would allow me to seamlessly enter and exit any given space. This gave me privileged views and insider scoops that most people never get to witness; it was a real eye opener. What this taught me was that it is impossible to know whether you truly "fit in" anywhere, because people prefer not to show their true feelings publicly. It became abundantly clear to me that I could never rely on other people's opinions of me to decide whether or not I felt I should be in any given space. Other people's perceptions are unreliable, unstable, untrustworthy, and sometimes illusory. The only gauge that you can really rely on for an honest assessment of your belonging is your own feeling of adeptness.

I gave myself the right to occupy any space I felt comfortable and confident occupying, and this confidence exuded an authority that very few dared challenge. Because of my linguistic abilities I was able to counter oppositions, and slowly became more secure in juggling plural identities despite incredulous and maligning looks. I refused to take my cues from others, and relied solely on my own belief in my absolute right to exist in whichever space I put myself. I was a smart-mouth!—a trait my mother wasn't particularly fond of, but I believe my father secretly admired.

By the age of seventeen I decided I no longer wanted to live in beautiful Switzerland because it felt like it catered to the wants and needs of wealthy tourists and occasional visitors more than its own inhabitants. Passersby counted for more than settlers, and being a settler left us seemingly forgotten and forsaken. Paradoxically, this made the older settlers extremely jealous of their claim on citizenship, and their disrespectful demeanor when someone happened to be blown in by the winds and attempted to put down roots in their beautiful field, left a bitter taste in my mouth. I longed for a place where people couldn't be misplaced, a place where my roots were undeniably deep, and nobody could declare sole ownership of what it meant to be a citizen.

Ironically, I sought refuge in my native Canada, where this injustice had been perpetrated onto my Mi'kmaq ancestors for centuries, despite their old roots. They were displaced within their own land. Shunned in their own territory. Expelled by the same people they had welcomed with open arms. Stripped of the very same wealth that they so willingly shared. Forced to feel shame in the very same knowledge they had used to save lives, and on which they had thrived for millennia. The contrast was palpable. I was constantly slipping—there for not being old enough, here for being too old.

We didn't have high schools on the Mi'kmaq Reserves in those days. We had to wake up at the break of dawn to be bussed into town to attend the nearest public school. I observed the Ulnoo (Native) kids huddling together in the staircase on the farthest wing of the enormous building, an area of the school the rest of the kids steered clear of as though it were a leper colony.

My classmates would watch me come in and out of the Ulnoo staircase, arms locked with one or two of my Rez friends, and pretend they didn't see me, only to take the first opportunity (usually in French immersion class) to inquire about my allegiances.

"Do you feel safe with them? Aren't you scared to live with them?"

To which I'd answer with curiosity, "Who is them?"

"You know... Indians."

"Why, don't you know, I'm Indian too? They're my cousins, my neighbors. We keep our doors open. We keep a pot of tea always on the stove for anyone who walks in. We all know each other. Of course I feel safe! I feel safer there than anywhere else! You should come over for tea some time!"

"Really?" they'd wonder, incredulous.

"Yeah... really! Haven't you ever been on a reserve?"

"Never!"

They never visited me on the reserve. They only invited me to parties where alcohol was abundant, perhaps thinking I'd feel right at home at a beer bash. I never went. The mere thought of it puzzled me to no end, and I knew I wouldn't enjoy it. We lost touch once school was over. They occasionally met my grandmother in town, and would inquire about me, but as soon as they heard I had converted to Islam, they lost all interest.

I lived on and off the Rez for four years, one full year during high school (which I chose to undergo to get used to learning and studying in English, despite having graduated from business school in Switzerland), and three others off and on. I spent summers, most weekends, and holidays on the Rez, and the rest of the year I stayed on campus at the university. There were many foreign students at this university, many of them Muslim, some Arab, but mostly Malaysian. Most Malaysian students studied business, which was my chosen field, given my background. So I got to spend a lot of time with them. I had a few friends from the Rez with me, but because of my attachment to Switzerland, I also had a yearning for the foreign spirit. Many people assumed I was a foreign student, and although I corrected them, I didn't mind, because I did feel a bit like a foreigner: I didn't grow up struggling between being an Ulnoo or an Aklasioq (white person). I was both; there was no tension between them inside of me, and this was weird for most people around me. So I joined all the foreign clubs I could join, even if I had no affiliation. I just wanted to balance out my awkwardness with others'. We would exchange stories, but even there, I wasn't rooted in Europe in the same way the foreign students were. I had no plans to return and finish my studies there. I was here to stay. They weren't. Their foreignness was only temporary. Mine was permanent.

I traveled to Toronto, Windsor, and Niagara Falls with the South East Asian Club, because the keeners among SEAC members wanted to look at their prospects for MBA studies. I was just going along for the ride, since I had already begun questioning whether I would be continuing in business.

During our stay in Toronto, I was treated to the most beautiful sight I had ever seen: the Muslim prayer. It was majestic. The people washed, quietly donned their white prayer garments over their regular clothes, lined up next to each other, and recited their barely audible prayers in unison, without once getting distracted by my gawking. I was mesmerized. I had never seen anything like this in my life, and I loved it! I immediately started asking about everything they did, and I decided there and then that I'd be fasting Ramadan with them. Upon my return, I continued quizzing all my Muslim friends about prayer, about their belief in God, about the place that Jesus (peace be upon him) played in their faith, about priests and imams, about marriage, divorce, about the other prophets. I spent the next couple of years re-evaluating everything, including my studies, and decided that my priorities needed reshuffling.

After a short visit to Switzerland once sophomore finals were over, I realized the only thing that would keep me there was my family. I purchased an English translation of the Qur'an and had begun reading, first sporadically, then methodically. I acquired other books on prayer, fasting, and the other pillars of Islam. I asked all the questions that popped into my mind, and I had a direct line to the sheikh of the largest mosque in the province, who was always happy to break everything down for me. By the time my senior year's fall classes began, I had converted, was praying five times a day, and was donning the hijab everywhere I went.

Islam was my new home, and to a large extent still is, although now I realize that my way of living Islam is different from everyone else's. It took me years to figure this out, a lot of trial and error, some disappointments, and more wake-up calls than I care to remember, but it's all been fruitful. I now realize that as much as similarities can unite us, differences can keep us in tune with our own unique rhythms and truths, circumstances and histories, and they need to be respected. Far from tearing us apart, they show us how we are meant to learn from each other, to grow and appreciate each other, rather than judge and exclude. Differences and similarities are mutually beneficial; we can't live without either, and the sooner we realize it, the better off we'll be.

Family is very important to me, and not being able to see them regularly always tugs at my heart like a dull ache. I have family on three different continents. I've lived with all of them, and I've felt at home with each of them. When heading to see them, the tug strengthens as soon as I approach the check-in counter at the airport, brimming with anticipation. I sit in my seat and watch my body being transported through the clouds as my mind drifts to and from the faces of the loved ones I temporarily left behind, and the ones whom I am about to temporarily join. It's like an out-of-body experience, filled with excitement and eagerness. Not even the thought of an accident distracts me from this feeling; the simple fact of having the freedom of mobility quells any discomfort. The choice to be able to move about and towards one loved one or the other is enough to sweep all fears under my little coach seat.

I've thought about the feelings I've had when I definitely didn't feel at home, and they were very few, but tremendously strong. Strong enough to make me want to escape. Strong enough to make me want to disappear. So strong, that I actually felt like part of me was dying. So strong, that I feared I might die at once. They occurred when I wasn't seen for who I am, and my efforts weren't recognized or were outwardly rejected as inconsequential. They occurred when no matter what I did or said, I was met with indifference, or worse, hypocrisy. They occurred when my inner self was so mercilessly attacked, ignored, maligned, or dismissed, that it began eroding. I'm a resilient, stubborn, strong person, but even I began doubting my role in this loveless place… to the point that I resolved never to return if I was ever able to escape it. Those memories and places are definitely not home to me.

I've thought about the feelings I've had when experiencing familiar, comfortable moments, with friends, or alone. It's a feeling of safety, of being able to be myself, of meeting appreciation and sharing mutual feelings of trust and respect, warmth and unconditional acceptance. But it doesn't have to emanate from others for it to feel like home; it just has to provide the opportunity to prove myself, to be able to demonstrate common ground, or common purpose. It needs to be open to the mere possibility.

This is why Canada feels like home to so many different people, because it allows for open dialogue, for interaction, for teaching and learning from each other, for growth and expansion of one's horizons, for the possibility of respectful disagreement. This isn't something you can obtain just anywhere, and although Canada has a larger dose of this magic combination than most other countries, it certainly doesn't mean it's perfect, or that it caters to everyone in equal measure. But its own self-awareness—of its indebtedness to the Mi'kmaq people, of its racist mistakes in the past, of its desire to stand alongside the U.S. while simultaneously distinguishing itself from it—allows for a great deal of flexibility in terms of arguments for accepting difference, and respect for civil disagreements.

They say home is where your heart is, but it's not true. It's just another one of those lies people keep repeating to try to convince themselves it's true, like "time heals all wounds," or "love springs eternal." Certainly not in my book. Home is a figment of our imaginations, and it reacts to, plays with, and interacts with our realities, to make them more or less bearable. It pushes us in and out of comfort zones, to seek out a quiet nook, to gather our thoughts at any given moment, to reconcile our differences, to make sense of the world "out there." Home is a state of mind that allows for space to be made in our lives for what matters to us. It's our reserve of strength, accumulated over years of experience and moments of relaxation; it is ready to pounce when called upon. It's constructed through the myriad filters our minds concoct, to protect us, shield us, and allow us respite before we go out and struggle some more, learn some more, become more. So it changes, through time, experience, and circumstance. It's a stable place in that it's accessible through the mind no matter where you are, but it's unstable in its concreteness.

This is the most remarkable aspect of home in my book: its transferability, its flexibility. Its fickleness is a blessing in disguise. Home is when, not where freedom and safety converge, when you are free to assent or dissent, to disperse or coalesce. Home is where you are free to change your mind. It's a box with a box-cutter, which you are able to use at will.

My home is in my mind. It's a memory, or millions of memories, which combine to remind me that I can do this, whatever this is. It's my little inner voice that tells me I'm who I think I am, no matter what anyone else says. It's a soft pat on the shoulder, a nudge under the table to speak up and watch out. It's a free hand offered to get up off the floor. Home is an act of self-affirmation, validation, and an exercise in assertiveness. Home is being true to who you know you are to your core.

Places only provide temporary reprieve from the limitations of society. Family and friends provide temporary relief from the frustrations stemming from lack of recognition for one's full self. But the limit is really only set internally.

I am my own home. I offer succor and temporary solace to the few who enter my embrace, but they too must find their own homes within themselves.

You can makeshift homes into safe havens for growth and nurturing, to provide memories, to allow for stability, knowing fully well that these are only temporary, illusory anchors in time. Questions, desires, aspirations will dare you to break out of any cocoon and break into flight. It's the nomadic curse that will endlessly call you to change, will urge you to pursue yet another dream, to expand your wingspan a bit more, to explore more territory, to chase another rainbow, and then to yearn for return once again. Those short moments of intersection in which growth and contentment coincide in a specific point before breaking apart, that's home. As soon as they touch, they lose their grip and continue their independent trajectories, obliging you to pursue your journey in search for yet another point of convergence. Again, and again, and again.

PART THREE:
HOME IS HERE

STANDING FOR WATER
TEHMINA KHAN

1979 and we are there all over again.
The seventh grader inside me
goes from ambiguous brown girl,
who has to explain that Indian means
being from India, to *Eye rain ian.*

To be Muslim is no longer just
avoiding pork at birthday parties,
it now makes me *Eye rain ian.*
Someone from *Eye ran.*
And they say *Eye ran* but don't know what it is or where,
or where India is for that matter,
and can anyone really find Santa Clara on a map?

Our neighborhood is white, black,
Mexican, and Filipino, and yet we
all try to erase ourselves when together,
silence the rhythms of our speech,
water down the flavors of our food,
hide our pain behind airbrushed masks,
and speak up only inside
the private sanctuary of our homes.

Eye ran, public enemy number one,
makes neighbors fly flags and yellow ribbons
in the faces of those who *do not belong.*
Soviet Union, USSR, not enemy but adversary,
worthy of being pronounced correctly,
an empire – strong but wrong,
and ugly, not beautiful like America.

The nightly news counts the days
that American hostages are held
by revolutionary students in Iran,
students who overthrew the tyrannical shah,
who years later will say maybe
it was a bad idea, taking hostages,
drunk on the power they held over the superpower.

Imam Khomeini is wise,
whisper grown up voices at
Indian Muslim dinner parties.
But he looks so mean, I think.
Islamic Republic — At last, a just society.
Mercy, Compassion… from God.
America cannot tell them what to do!

I get used to hiding in shadows
while flags of the citizenship imposed
by my birthplace are raised up high,
smothering the words that connect us to home.
You will be assimilated, resistance is futile.

I leave Santa Clara for Berkeley,
where we build shantytowns to protest apartheid,
march against United States' proxy wars
in Central America, organize for a free Palestine,
and feel the political become personal.
Caffeinated and armed with words,
we raise our voices, silencing fear.

When I help elderly immigrants prepare for
citizenship interviews, I tell them America is not beautiful,
and its power is ugly, but here you are, so be here,
and live here, and speak your stories and your language,
keep your grandchildren close, and tell them
who you are... who they are.

And 2017 is 1979, is Japanese Internment,
is the Chinese Exclusion Act, is Jim Crow Segregation,
is every treaty broken with First Nations.
But 2017 is also Sanctuary,
five centuries of resistance,
and all of us standing up for Standing Rock.
And we stand in the shadows
of a settler colony that wants us assimilated or gone.
But we walk in our own light,
as we weave our voices together into
a multicolored tapestry.
And speak a symphony of languages,
mathematical equations,
stories, prayers
to each other,
to the Divine
for water... for the water inside all of us.

HOME IS HERE
KELLY IZDIHAR CROSBY

One day someone one asked me,
"Do you feel comfortable living as a Muslim in America?"
And I really had to give it some thought.
Because the question, while painfully relevant, felt so odd.
Because I can't imagine feeling uncomfortable in my own home.

'Cuz this is my land
And I refuse to let anyone make me feel unwelcome in my own home.
I'm African-American, a Black woman, born and raised, in New Orleans.
My African, Spanish and French roots run deep like the bayou,
As long as the Mississippi.

My ancestors built this house called America,
Paid for it with their bodies, bones, and unpaid labor.

You see, some of my ancestors,
Kidnapped, shackled and shipped to this land,
Were Muslims,
Millions of souls, millions of believers,
With *La ilaha illa Allah* carved upon their hearts.

Islam ain't some foreign import.
It's been here. *We've* been here.
And you can thank European slave traders for that.

Those men and women who prayed *fajr* at the break of dawn
Out of the overseer's sight,
Hidden to protect themselves from the sting of the master's whip.
And those devotees who observed the holy month of Ramadan, while
   slaving away,
With only table scraps and bitter tears to break their fast.

Days cutting sugar cane, picking cotton and tobacco,
Nights spent in silent reflection, yearning for their homelands.

For those literate slaves, writing in Arabic script,
The prayers and lessons from their *madrassa*,
On stolen scraps of paper and the walls of their shacks,
All in secret.

The men and women of modesty and humility,
Stripped of their colorful robes and headwraps,
Paraded and degraded on auction blocks, to be prodded and fondled
   like cattle.
No... worse than an animal.

Ask AbdurRahman ibn Sori and Yarrow Mamout,
And Estavanico, Yusef bin Ali, and Omar bin Syed.
And the Gullah Guchee of South Carolina and Georgia.
And the Senegambia Muslims who cultivated the land of Louisiana.
Hell, you can even ask Thomas Jefferson about his copy of the Qur'an.
And ask John Adams and see his signature on the Treaty of Tripoli.

How could I be uncomfortable?
I *refuse* to be uncomfortable.
They have suffered more than enough discomfort for me.
Their sacrifices are the wellspring of my strength.
Their example of piety and fortitude amid one of the greatest crimes
    in human history
Makes a racist neighbor wearing a MAGA hat look very, very small.
My ancestors carved out a home in the bitter wildness,
Hostile, unfriendly and apathetic to their suffering.

Modern-day anti-Muslim sentiment is bad. But I can cope.
I can be firm in my resolve, in my multiple identities.
This is my *home*. For better, and as history has shown, for the worst.
It's my home, with warts and all.
This nation is my inheritance I claim by birthright.

And for their sake,
I will live,
Shine, breathe,
Believe,
In this *deen*.
Unapologetically.

AFRICAN AMERICAN MUSLIM FEMALE —
OR HOW I EMBRACED ISLAM AND BECAME A SUPERHERO
GAIL KENNARD

As an African-American convert, I embraced Islam as the best religious practice for me. Like many converts, I made a choice and was zealous about my new religion. Through my experiences meeting Muslim-American immigrants, I found they sometimes had the same zeal about America as I had about Islam. They or their parents or grandparents made a choice to come to America. Often in flight from authoritarian Muslim governments, some had a less zealous opinion of the religion. They knew the ways Islam has been subverted for political, economic and social power abroad, and how Muslims have fallen short. I knew America as a native and as a person of color. My enslaved African ancestors were not immigrants by choice. I knew how Americans have subverted the nation's higher values for political, economic and social power for centuries. Americans have fallen short.

Today we are two sides of the same coin—me, as one who adopted Islam, and they, as those who adopted America. Both of us have made decisions to change either our faith or our homeland. Together I believe we can change both Islam and America. To do that, we must become superheroes in America, and I am one of them. Not fearful of setting ambitious goals, I decided to work in two areas, one external and one internal: (1) to counter Islamophobia against Muslims, and (2) to improve the practice of my religion for all Muslims in America, especially women.

Let me start with the first area. For the past twenty-five years, a rise in Islamophobia has led to advocacy and activism by American Muslims. Because I was born here and have lived here as a member of a subordinate group, African Americans, I believe I know American culture well. Muslims, like African Americans, are a subordinate group in America. Given my background, I decided that I can be a bridge between Muslim and non-Muslim Americans to counter Islamophobia.

I decided to join the board of a non-profit organization dedicated to serving the needs of people who are homeless in Los Angeles. It is not led by Muslims, nor were any Muslims on the board. I was attempting to follow the Qur'anic commandments to be active in good deeds and gain the pleasure of Allah by helping others. Seeing the rising numbers of my fellow citizens living in squalor on the streets, many of them people of color, moved me to want to do something about this problem. I grew up watching Wonder Woman, Batman, Superman and all the superheroes who rescue citizens in distress. This was my first opportunity to be a superhero.

Through serving on the board of directors and as its president for one term, I was able to interact with others who are not Muslim. In these interactions, I did not wear my Islam "on my sleeve," but I did wear headscarves and modest clothing. (I found this was also helpful in covering up my superhero cape.) I also excused myself from eating during the day during Ramadan, and everyone on the board knew that I was Muslim, the only one at that time.

I got to know the board members well enough that soon after the 9/11 attacks, I decided I would host an interfaith *iftar* (fast-breaking meal during Ramadan) at my home. I invited some of my Muslim friends, both converts and immigrants, to be with Christians, Jews, and other friends of no faith. It was an opportunity to dispel myths about who Muslims are and what we believe. I was surprised that not only were the Christians and Jews learning about Islam, but one of the Muslims told me that she had never been in a home where Jewish people were present.

Several years after that, one of my Jewish colleagues from the board of the homeless organization told me something that affirmed that what I was doing was having at least a small impact. He told me that he had told his Jewish friends and family about me and that Muslims are not what they think. I thanked him for sharing his experience and for countering misconceptions and prejudice about Muslims in the Jewish community. Then I joked that I hoped he told them that I hadn't strapped any explosives around my waist nor set off any car bombs since I have known him (or ever).

Since then I have participated in interfaith groups with other Muslim superheroes because I feel it is important that non-Muslims know at least one Muslim who they can go to for questions about Islam. In many cases, Christians and Jews have told me they have never talked to a Muslim or don't know any Muslims. Some have also said that after meeting Muslims, they have spoken up when family and friends make inaccurate statements about Islam and Muslims.

This work is not easy, and sometimes it is uncomfortable. Hundreds of times we are asked about terrorism and why Muslims don't condemn terrorist acts (we do, hundreds of times). But answering these questions is necessary. It requires the Qur'anic attributes of constancy and patience. Unless Muslims build coalitions and relationships with those of other faiths and across the racial divide, Islamophobia will continue to grow. I don't think we have a choice. Literally, our lives are at risk.

According to the Pew Research Center, the number of assaults against Muslims in the United States has risen beyond the level that followed the 2001 attacks. Based on FBI data, Pew reports that Muslim and Jewish people were the two most common targets of hate crimes, making up fifty-four percent. The FBI reports that hate crimes increased nearly five percent in 2016, some 6,100 incidents.

Incidents of hate crimes, vandalism and mosque burnings in California, Texas, Missouri and other states have increased. The Council on American Islamic Relations reported seventy-eight incidents of mosque vandalism and burnings in 2015, up from twenty incidents in 2014.

The greatest threat is from white supremacists. Despite the fear mongering of those spreading Islamophobia about Muslim terrorists, according to the Southern Poverty Law Center, there are now 954 hate groups in the United States. Between 2014 and 2016, the number grew from 784 to 917. Some seventy-five percent of the terrorist attacks in the United States since 9/11 have been committed by white extremists. Christian Picciolini, a writer and former member of America's first white-power skinhead hate group, wrote in the *Los Angeles Times* that "if these extremists had brown skin, we would call them terrorists."

Given this threat, I believe I have a responsibility to stand up for those who are victimized by these attacks wherever and whenever they occur. I could fall into despair. Despite my small efforts, Islamophobia and hate crimes are rising. Likewise, despite my small efforts with the non-profit, homelessness is ten times higher than when I first joined the organization. But defeat is not an option. My faith dictates that I persevere. And I am a superhero, right? Superheroes don't give up.

On Friday, November 2, 2018, I joined Muslims, Christians and others for Shabbat services at a local synagogue to show support for the Jewish community after the killings by an anti-Semitic gunman in Pittsburgh. Some of these Jewish congregants had come to our mosque to support us after President Trump issued the Muslim travel ban in 2017. Both of these times, I have felt embraced for being both American and Muslim. In tragedy, there is also light.

I was also heartened by the number of Muslims who have run for public office all over the country and won seats at the local, state and national level. For the first time, two Muslim women are members of the U.S. Congress, and there are many more elected to city offices, school boards, state legislatures and judgeships. These women and men have been elected by majority non-Muslim electorates, so this is encouraging; America is showing that Islamophobia can be overcome.

Ilhan Omar of Minnesota, who wears a headscarf, is the first Muslim to do so in the U.S. Congress. She is a role model for all Muslim women across the country who have been discouraged, either from fear or pressure, from wearing their headscarves. My hope is that now Muslim women and girls will feel a little more empowered. In declaring her victory in the election, she said that Minnesota doesn't just welcome immigrants, it sends them to Congress. In a time of heightened Islamophobia and hate, there is light. There are superheroes among us.

My second objective, to have an impact on the practice of Islam in America, is equally important and difficult. I mentioned my knowing American culture well. What I do not know well are Muslim cultural practices abroad.

Walking through the streets of Mecca when I made the pilgrimage, I observed signs written in restaurants declaring "No women allowed." As an African American, my mind flashed back to the segregation that occurred in the South under Jim Crow laws. Blacks were not allowed in public restaurants, theaters and other places—segregation based on skin color, not gender. My attraction to Islam was like Malcolm X's, who famously wrote in his autobiography that when he visited Mecca, the racial divide was invisible. Black-skin and white-skin Muslims praying together. No color line in Islam, but what about gender?

For me, as a female, those signs prohibiting service to women in Mecca were unforgettable. Seeing the segregation of women in public places in Muslim cultures challenged me to think about the status of women in Islamic practice when I returned home to the United States. As a new convert, I was reluctant to challenge the status quo—that women were separated during the prayer, and that women, for the most part, were not given a voice in the Muslim community equivalent to that of men. I was told that women could not give *khutbahs* (sermons) or lead prayer in mixed gender settings because men must have something that is uniquely theirs. Women are given the exclusive gift of being mothers, a greater gift than leadership in the community. Men cannot give birth and Prophet Muhammad said that Muslims should give honor to their mother above their father. I was told that this was the trade-off—along with the desire for modesty and not being distracted during prayer—that justified the exclusion of women's voices and segregation. I did not challenge the status quo. Reflecting now, those arguments were not persuasive, but at the time, I did not have the knowledge of Islamic history nor the courage to speak up. My superhero powers failed me on this one.

But in the past decade, Muslim women have slowly been challenging these segregation practices. In 1994, Islamic scholar Amina

Wadud delivered a *khutbah* in Cape Town, South Africa, and later in 2005, before a mixed-gender gathering in New York. At the same prayer service, another woman performed the call to prayer, also a previously male role. Their actions were widely condemned but also supported by a few male Islamic scholars. I remember hearing about her historic *khutbah* and sharing the news with other women at the mosque I attended. None of them felt the way I did, that this was a positive development. At the time, there was minimal grassroots support for change from Muslim women themselves.

Then in 2007, Muslims for Progressive Values was formed by a Malaysian-born woman performer and activist, Ani Zonneveld, in Los Angeles, that organized women-led mixed-gender prayer services. This group, with a mission to advance human rights and inclusion, has expanded throughout the United States and abroad. However, its focus is on social justice principles more than religious practice.

In 2015, a younger generation of women, led by Hasna Masnavi and others from both immigrant and convert backgrounds, decided to start the Women's Mosque of America in Los Angeles. It is an exclusive space for women, following the format of the traditional Friday prayer service but with all functions led by women. Men are not allowed. In addition, it welcomes all sects within Islam—Sunni, Shi'a, and Sufi, as well as women from other faiths. There is broad diversity in race, ethnicity, national origin, age, socio-economic status, and education.

My initial reaction was that men needed to hear what women have to say just as much as women need to hear other women's voices. But these young women, in the generation after Amina Wadud, saw a need for a place where women can reinforce their Islamic faith, and they could not wait for it, nor could they believe that the mixed-gender mosques would or could accommodate them. The men who want to hear what the women are saying, I was told, could access the *khutbahs* posted online. Additionally, the Women's Mosque of America was not intended to replace the existing mixed-gender mosques. Gatherings of the Women's Mosque are held once a month, not weekly, as are the existing mixed-gender congregations, nor are they held at a mosque. Mormon, Unitarian and Jewish meeting halls have leased space to the

Women's Mosque. Once they met in a 'pop-up' space in a retail store in a shopping center.

A consistent number of women have been attending the services, some traveling great distances from out of the city, state and abroad. Some say they felt unwelcomed, uninspired or uncomfortable at the existing mosques and stopped attending them, or never attended in the first place. It is also safe for transgender and lesbian women who feel uncomfortable in many existing mosques. The dress policy is "come as you are." There are no requirements about appropriate dress. Headscarves are optional, although most women wear a head covering during the prayer itself. The mosque is intended to be a safe, non-judgmental place to express their faith.

The topics covered at the Women's Mosque range from Islamic practices like prayer, fasting and charity to mental health, marriage, divorce, domestic abuse, sexual assault, and civic engagement. Women have spoken about re-examining Qur'anic verses from a woman's perspective and affirming the Qur'an's guidance.

In August 2015, I delivered a *khutbah* at the Women's Mosque, and I have delivered several others since then. Being a *khateebah* (sermon giver) has changed my connection to my faith in ways that I cannot articulate. I am grateful for this experience, and I have found the voice that I suppressed when I returned from my pilgrimage to Mecca and saw the "No women allowed" signs. Thanks to these pioneering women, my superhero mojo was revived in a new setting, amongst Muslims.

Unlike mixed-gender services, at the close of the *khutbah* and prayer, women form a circle and can make comments or ask questions of the woman who gave the *khutbah*. One of the most powerful circles occurred after a *khutbah* about the speaker's own experience as a victim of sexual abuse from within her family. Numerous women related their own #MeToo experiences, and the affirmation that followed was transformational for many. Through delivering *khutbahs*, reciting the call to prayer, and participating in the circle, the emphasis is on giving women an opportunity to be heard. Women, often socialized not to speak, are encouraged to use the opportunity to practice speaking up and giving voice to their experiences in a non-threatening space.

Since the Women's Mosque started, there has been a noticeable improvement in how women have been received at some local mosques. Several years ago, the Islamic Center of Southern California, one of the more inclusive congregations in the nation, began hosting side-by-side prayers for the two annual *Eid* (Islamic holiday) prayers and at some of its services held in satellite facilities. In this way, women and men have equal access to the man giving the *khutbah*. This is a model that may be followed in other parts of the country. Women at the Islamic Center are also part of the rotating slate of speakers who give commentary before the evening prayers during Ramadan, and women have served on the board of the center for decades. Recently, a woman was elected as the center's board chair, a first. These changes move us in the right direction.

But this inclusiveness is not typical. I recently visited a mosque in another city for Friday prayer. When traveling, Muslim women must navigate the unknown boundaries of where they can pray. Sometimes there is a separate room, a basement, upstairs area, or an outside building designated for women; sometimes women are not allowed at all. But unless you know someone who can tell you the local protocols, women, especially those traveling alone, can be at a loss. During the Jim Crow era in the South, black travelers relied on what is called the "Green Book" that listed all the places where they could safely stop for gas, food, and lodging, because many public accommodations were closed to blacks. When I visit a mosque in an unfamiliar place, I wish I had a "Green Book" for Muslim women. Muslim-American women must redefine worship spaces that nurture their spiritual needs.

As I mentioned, as an African American and a Muslim, I have moved between both Muslim and non-Muslim worlds. I have also moved between predominantly African-American and immigrant Muslim communities. Though there has been some movement towards bringing these two groups together, for the most part, they worship separately. I am asked if I have experienced racism from immigrant communities in which I am active. The answer is "yes,"

I have experienced both racism and sexism. Immigrant Muslims are not immune from the racism and sexism that pervades our culture. Similarly, I have experienced African-American Muslims expressing prejudice towards immigrant Muslims. One psychologist made the analogy that racism is like 'smog.' Everyone breathes it in and no one escapes. Another psychologist explained this as an example of "hurt people hurting other hurt people."

African Americans embraced Islam for very different reasons than immigrant Muslims. Islamic practice among African Americans and immigrant Muslims will necessarily reflect those different motivations and the needs of their respective constituencies. As Islamic practice evolves in the American context, both groups will decide what works best for them, each will recognize that they can learn from each other, and these communities in America will change over time. Both communities are increasingly realizing that they have common struggles—law enforcement killings of unarmed black men, the mass incarceration of black and brown people, hate crimes, the detention of brown, black and Muslim refugees by immigration enforcement, and the domestic war on terror. These issues are clearly interconnected.

In conclusion, those who work for social change have learned that it is often a good strategy to advocate with an eye not only on what you are against, but more importantly, what kind of future you can envision. I am heartened by the growing number of Muslim-American superheroes from all backgrounds who are working on change, both within the larger American society and within the Muslim community. My vision is for a future where:

— Addressing racism, sexism and Islamophobia, their effects and high costs to our society, will have the same urgency as the national effort to send a man to the moon was in the 1960s;

— White supremacists, anti-Semites, Islamophobics, anti-LGBTQ, misogynists, xenophobes, and other extremists with non-inclusive views will be reformed, and their past actions will only be found in history books;

- Sexual harassment, abuse, and assault will be rare, and when they occur, victims' rights will be respected by law enforcement, the courts, and in public opinion;
- It will be unremarkable that the voice of Muslim women is heard in all arenas of American life;
- Decisions about how women dress and their reproductive choices will be free from governmental and any other external interference;
- Women's voices will be heard from the mosque *minbar* (pulpit) and in leadership in mosques across the nation;
- And no woman who wants to enter a mosque for prayer or a service will have to wonder if she will be welcomed.

Unrealistic? Un-Islamic?
Calling all superheroes to report for duty.
Lots to do.

FORMULATING A HISTORY
KRISTEN OBARSKY

A summer investigating cemeteries embedded images of toppled tombstones into my childhood memories. My mom, a genealogy guru, dedicated three or four solid months one year to serious sleuthing into the lives of our ancestors to compile our family's history in America. She carted us kids around to cemeteries, historical societies, and to the homes of close and distant relatives in her avid search for lost parts of the narrative, and data that would illuminate her own history and life. After her research, she wrote short stories about those family members who had played a pivotal part in the overall adventure of our emigration to the U.S., and thoughtfully gathered those stories into a protective, 'groovy' 1970s mustard-yellow binder. I am the inheritor of this collection, adding to it and making my own history.

"Genealogy is addictive," my mother once confessed to me. We all have our addictions and my mother's started in her thirties when her Aunt Ro shared stories of our ancestors who came over on the Mayflower in the early 17th century. This piqued my mom's interest and, later, after watching the powerful TV miniseries *Roots* in the 1970s, her addiction deepened. The striking storytelling of *Roots,* highlighting the history of a slave, impacted her deeply. My mother wanted to record our family history in a similar, imaged way: dynamic, rich and soulful, with a mix of good and bad. She dedicated much time and energy to piecing together a vivid picture of our history. The final results were textual, visual and tactile. After finishing writing the genealogical short stories, my mother created a quilt to represent each one of their protagonists. It is another physical object symbolizing our lineage and memorializing our ancestors.

Frequent graveyard explorations for kids is a bit unusual, but the familiarity of spending time in these spaces has had a lasting impact on the adult I have become. To me, cemeteries are not scary, haunted or even sad. They are, instead, places to gather stories and information, a way to learn about others who have passed on before you. In learning about your ancestors and lineage, you learn about yourself. It provides an opportunity to reflect on what you will and wish to leave behind as your own legacy.

My mother's research, performed before the onset of the internet and Ancestry.com, faced many hurdles due to the frequent changes in name or location of many relatives. Despite this challenge, she faced the daunting task with love and enthusiasm. After the rigors of research and the endless scanning of old newspapers as well as birth, death, and marriage certificates, she ended up having curated a pleasant and endearing family chronology. Most early American family histories possess a default optimistic and cheerful storyline. Who would have wanted to document having had a hard year in which they faced near starvation, poverty, or failed enterprises and endeavors? This would have brought shame to their name and family, especially to those who left their home country behind to build a better and more successful life. Falling short of what came to be called the American Dream would have been too humiliating to admit. Our family history was itself a mainly rosy picture of pioneers, Puritans, farmers, and factory workers, with a few secrets sprinkled throughout that would reveal themselves only centuries later. I still claim these physical ancestors as part of my own lineage and remain inspired by their work ethic and dogged determination.

During my mother's summer of genealogical exploration, the three of us kids aged five, seven, and nine, were along for the ride, whether we liked it or not. During those hot months, we travelled all across the green rolling hills of Pennsylvania's countryside. I still remember the way the humidity settled down in the valleys. The plants and trees looked listless in the high heat, and the dragonflies zipped about and greeted us. We would park along the side of the road, immersed in the density of white Queen Anne's lace and yellow ragweed. The pungent perfumes of pollen permeated the air. We were my mother's little assistants as she documented her gravestone findings. Often holding her tracing paper over the gravestones or her charcoal that she used for rubbings, I was more haunted by nursing home visits than cemetery ones. A part of her research included meeting and greeting loads of elderly family members and friends. I remember trying not to gawk at the hunched, fragile, little bodies in wheelchairs. Like all mothers, my mother was smart, and she fed us myriad candied distractions like lollipops, chocolates, or gum, that kept us from complaining and kept our wanting-to-gape jaws closed. It made the ancestral summer a sticky, sweet and sour experience.

Recently historians have filled in a few missing pieces of our history, publishing detailed accounts online of our very first ancestor, Edward Doty, who sailed to America on the Mayflower. The findings were juicy, even unsavory. We had always claimed that our ancestors were mild-mannered, sweet souls looking for religious freedom. This is because a majority of the passengers on the Mayflower were religious reformers, Puritans, seeking breathing room to practice a different version of Protestantism. Edward Doty travelled this voyage on the Mayflower as an indentured servant, a man who had to work for a set term and who, only once released from the contract, was free to marry, acquire lands or do business. The Mayflower leaders were probably strict about who was going to join this community, only allowing Puritans. But most likely Mr. Doty was looking more for economic than religious freedom. He must have been in a desperate financial situation if he decided or was forced to sign on as an indentured servant rather than as a free man. According to the new online accounts, a collection of jail and court records expose Mr. Doty's life of fighting, fraud, and theft after his release from servitude. Archival documents describe Edward Doty, for example, as having "engaged in a sword and dagger duel . . . made regular appearances in Plymouth Colony Court . . . twice for assault, once for theft, and once for slander."

Another early relative is on record for her "unladylike conduct," while her dad was said to have performed "mischief with Maydes and women." Still another gambled away the family farm. But we were not all deadbeats. We only count a few outlaws among the overwhelming number of hardworking and dedicated folks composing our now centuries-long existence in the U.S. Outwardly, this troublesome Mr.

Edward Doty appears to form the cornerstone of the whole family's American genealogy, and the new revelations of his lawlessness don't make me feel any different about my ancestors. I can claim who I want as my forebears, hold on to the good, while letting go of the bad. I am also learning that I have more ancestors now than ever: spiritual ancestors, those who don't share the same DNA, but who share the same religious unity, the belief in the oneness of God.

I appreciate a lot about my mother's family genealogy project. The main thing is that it made me reflect on my own history. Where do I belong now in this continuum of people? Do I even belong in this story of American ancestors, now that I have converted to Islam, form part of a minority, and feel like an outsider?

Before I became Muslim, I was never really troubled by the family members in our genealogical record who changed their 'ethnic' surname to something more 'American.' There was an enormous amount of name changing, explaining why American genealogy is so messy. For example, my infamous Edward Doty ancestor could also have spelled his last name as Doten, Dotey, Doughty, or Doughtey, and records show all of these names being used at some point. There was a Clark who was previously Clarke. We have a Boney that was a Bonney, Bani, Bonye, or Boniface. Baumgardner could also be Bomgardner or Bumgardener. My own last name was changed from Okbarsky to Obarsky. But now, as an American convert, my eyes have been opened to those name changes. I see them as witnesses to the pressure to assimilate. Compromise for the sake of the majority has thus existed since the era of the earliest settlers and has continued on until today.

The family story also discusses an ancestor who changed her religious denomination for something more mainstream. Because I don't know the full story, I am unaware whether the shift from Greek Orthodox to Roman Catholic was due to social pressure or personal reasons. Now a Muslim, I have a stronger connection to those immigrant families who faced complicated decisions regarding faith or family name, not knowing if assimilative blending in with the majority would give them true satisfaction. I feel more linked because I understand the dilemma of wanting to belong, but also wanting to be rooted firmly in one's own personal identity. I have a surge of sympathy for them, wondering if their surrendering of their identity, name or faith, just to feel accepted in this land of freedom, was necessary or not. I relate to the emotions provoked by feeling like an outcast. I wonder if their fear of the unknown and the move to a foreign land heightened a perhaps unnecessary anxiety.

There have been a few occurrences in my life when someone looked at my scarf and thought that I don't understand English, or times when someone gave me a condescending, unfriendly glare. There are also times when people call me traitor or other strong words not worth repeating. These occasions are remarkably infrequent, with 99% of interaction with fellow citizens being respectful, hospitable, and surprisingly graceful. I shouldn't be surprised by kindness, but it does catch me off guard. It is not fair or healthy to assume everyone hates you, because they don't. People are mostly concerned with their own issues. I wonder if my ancestors knew this: that they didn't need to let fear of the unknown muddle their thinking, but instead could simply ease into America and not worry about how others perceived them. Looking for others' approval is futile. People are fickle and moody, and it is better to look at a continuously merciful and loving God for security and approval.

Racism or Islamophobia is unfortunately real and we all deal with it differently. As an adult who is more secure in my identity and has studied my faith thoroughly, I feel grounded and able to handle what comes my way. I will add that I am living in a state which is known for its niceness, and I am truly fortunate; others have it much worse and face daily struggles with Islamophobia. However, I have been extremely nervous about my small children who are in a society where racist undercurrents sometimes find their way to the surface. My children do not have a full grasp of self-esteem or identity yet. How are they supposed to defend their faith when they still know so little of it? My heart is deeply affected by cases of kids who are bullied because of race, religion, or socioeconomic status. To protect my own kids, I have been homeschooling them. I'm not ready for them to be a target until

I know they understand their faith. I'm not saying homeschooling is for everyone, but without any extended family in our state, this is our solution: strengthening our nuclear family, creating a positive identity, and when the kids are mature enough to articulate their faith, then we might start to explore other avenues in education.

In reflecting back on my experiences in which I was made to feel like an outcast, they did sting at the time, but I always ask forgiveness for the culprits and ask for myself to not hold onto ill feeling. I'm thankful I have a solid faith to support me and keep me strong. My faith keeps me from being distracted or traumatized by my direct experience with Islamophobic acts. I don't feel I need to prove my "Americanness" like my ancestors did. What is the point? It is never enough for some. No matter how much you love camping, baseball, fishing, steak and potatoes, it is not enough "Americanness." You can have a history from America's birth, and people will still call you un-American.

It took becoming a minority to really value history and who I am. Now I have to dig deep, to pray more and pull from my physical and spiritual ancestors who, like me, kept plodding along even when things didn't go according to their plan. I have to trust there is a greater plan that God has carefully selected for me. Because I'm a minority, I feel elevated. God chose me to be one of his followers from all the billions of people.

I do hold a place in the continuum of my lineage. I want to take charge of my own history and have ownership of my story. I take it back, both reclaiming what is good, and sidestepping the bad. We cannot choose our family, forefathers, or other people adhering to our faith, but we can choose our actions and what to do today and tomorrow. My faith has pushed me to be courageous and brave. It takes tremendous fortitude to walk into a grocery store, not knowing if insults will be hurled my way. For myself, I am proud that I have to have the tenacity to do something that others in my family were not able to do: stand up for my faith, remain unwavering and not change an ounce. Islam has distinguished me in a noble cause and held me up firmly. I will stand tall and refuse to compromise my commitment to my religious tradition. I want this to be my history and my legacy. From now on, I decide where I belong. My freedom is in my hands.

My mother's project, now technically completed, still requires updating: adding newspaper clippings, pictures, marriage, birth, death, and divorce records. The once neat organized binder now overflows with several loose sheets of paper shoved into it, and looks disheveled. This is history: messy, changing, and growing every day. Our actions today are a part of history. Right now, we can change those family histories into what we want. My mother, by creating her binder and her quilt representing fifty-six chosen family stories, transformed history into something tangible and accessible. Imagine having a cozy warm blanket of the history you choose to keep you warm on chilly nights. She picked only these fifty-six stories to delineate her personal history, and we too can make our own history however we want. It feels symbolic, this history quilt. It is pleasing to think your history can be your comfort, can keep you secure. Imagine slipping under that blanket after a challenging day, sleeping soundly under a quilted fabric of history. Toasty, calming, relaxing, let it soothe you. Let it absorb your tears. Let the blanket become molded over your tired body, enshroud you, and diffuse your stresses. Let it be soft and malleable, never stiff or inflexible.

I might be of Irish or Slovak ancestry because of some shared DNA and facial features, but what really courses through my veins now is submission. I am choosing my spiritual ancestors from the lineage and tribes of those great men and women who held fast in the face of danger or ridicule: Noah, Jesus, Mary and Moses, and all the other devotees of God. They were the brave and proud. They didn't change for any other human beings. They were minorities among the masses of people, and they didn't get caught up in fear about what people were thinking of them. My new history is of my choosing: piety, protection, pride and promise. I decide where I belong. I belong to God; the rest is just human history.

QN. HILL
ARWA ABOUON

Fast food nation that is America!?
No, you are variety
all the way around to Africa.
You burst like Tapioca.
You're comforting like Moussaka.
You are natural as Mastika.
You and Everything with a hint of Paprika.
There is this dish from this guy's country, Kaká?
Let's not go there, forget the Vodka.
You are a warm cup of Arabica.
You are my favorite TomKha.
I'm sorry I burnt the chicken Tikka,
but it's okay because next feast is in Mecca.

THE RETURN
A. M. HASSAN

Here I am, just three stops from getting off in the downtown I used to know so well. I close my eyes, wanting to take in the chatter around me, the leaning and lurching of the train. I open them to follow the path of leaves blowing outside, allow myself to guess where they might end up. The warm life of the train car is left behind as I step off and into the coldness of the afternoon. Standing in the station, I stop short of talking to strangers, knowing the house will be full of enough of them. I think to call my cousin, the one who begged me to be here, and ask for a ride, but I head out to find a cab instead of looking for more ways to waste time. I try hard to feel what I used to feel in this town, anything to remove the unease itching my mind, but nothing brings back the old cheer. As the coconut-scented cab weaves through familiar streets, I try again to distract myself from the fact that I now have less than ten minutes to come up with why I've stayed away for so long.

Mona answers the door, and her cool gaze quickly goes from my face to the burgundy scarf around my head. Her words from the last time we spoke chime in my memory, blotting out all the good times we had when we still treated each other like sisters. *You're so weird now, it's like I don't know you.* My decision to grow a backbone and move away had cracked the bonds of our family, but my change in faith had shattered what was left. She had been the most outspoken, calling over and over to say I was crazy and confused, as if she really cared in the first place. Every long dead battle had resurrected itself with new life and a new cause until I became the source of all family discord and scorn, taking her place as the damned one. My stammered defenses only earned cruelty. *I don't want to know someone like you.* The anger in her eyes couldn't be forgotten, and I'd set off for my final year of undergrad with the intention to stay gone for a while, not thinking years would go by so fast.

Our hug is no more than a light pressing of hands on each

other's backs as I move around her to find our mother. The smell of nutmeg and apples fills the house, along with that of meat, the kind I won't eat. I remember the tuna sandwich I'd thought was too ridiculous to bring to a family dinner, but now I wish I'd out-thought myself. *You know no one's going to cater to you,* Mona had said when I mustered the courage to let her know I was coming, an olive branch thrown back in my face. She didn't care if I did or didn't come: either way, there would be no special trip to any special grocery store. There *would* be plenty of peanut butter and jelly if need be—our mother was half-serious when she added that to the background of the conversation, never getting on the phone herself. Now she is standing in front of the sink with her hands deep in bathing collard greens. Her smile is real.

"Tenelle baby!" Her hug is full, but quick. She hadn't thought I'd really show up. "You still wearin' that thing?"

"Yeah, it's been a couple years now, Ma."

"Oh yeah?" Her initial smile drops, her voice lowering to the warning tone I know all too well. "Well, we wouldn't know. Ain't seen you in so long."

Suddenly, I feel like the skittish girl I'd left here as, my tongue tied, my reasons sounding as lame as they probably are. Aloud, 'being busy' didn't sound like a real reason at all. One is never really too busy for 'family,' unless something important is missing. We had love, but it was a strange kind of love that left you sore and worn down at the end of the day, the kind you had to take in small doses, lest you be put low forever. For my whole life, I'd always wanted to say how I couldn't stand the way they made me feel. It had only gotten worse since now what I wore and ate could be used against me. One shouldn't have to fear coming home; it shouldn't be the one place where you have to cross your arms, hoping to prevent anyone from picking apart your soul. I'd always wanted to ask to be taken seriously, but it was never the time or place. Besides, that very request would be an invitation for ridicule. Maybe it *was* my fault, like they'd said so many times; maybe *I* had made everything all too 'weird.' Maybe I *had* become too 'serious,' too 'sensitive.' I want to drop my arms, relax, but can't even force it as I look awkwardly around to see what I can help with. The moment passes before I can say anything real. My mother is silent again, like I hadn't said anything at all.

The house fills with laughter and bodies, making a corner of the living room my refuge and the only spot holding one person. Most recognize me and speak cautiously, unsure whether or when to bring up my old problems. My past is still hung up in the air like cobwebs for all to see and judge, and to cause confusion when put next to the image of me now. A former friend of mine clings to my sister and, together, they form an invisible wall to keep me out. I can't even remember why the girl and I stopped talking, but it doesn't matter anymore. I look away, ignoring her efforts to cut me with her eyes. I try to stop fiddling with the ends of my scarf, stop looking as if I need someone to say, "You're doing ok. I'm proud of you."

I feel shame realizing that in all this time away, and with all the things I've achieved, building myself up stronger in their absence, here I am still aching for a pat of approval that isn't coming. A pat that never comes for any reason, to any of us, that I can recall. The cousin who promised to stick with me hasn't turned up. I am told by her mother, my aunt, that she's traded our Thanksgiving for the one at her boyfriend's parents' house. I don't blame her, and I don't bother to call, knowing she won't pick up, even if I call fifty times.

The table fits us all, voices loud and soft coming together to make lively noise. The air is tense as always, each person wondering who knows what about them, and if they'll be roasted as entertainment. My own voice finds no ears to pour into, unless I am willing to dodge the usual bullets: Where have I been? And what the hell am I wearing? Is this what I 'do' in New York? An uncle asks me these questions as if he has never asked before, a bigger audience making him forget. My mother is sitting too near *not* to cut in.

"I said the same thing," she laughs, like she is suddenly unaware of my frailty, my need for her alliance. "It's too hot for all that. I just don't see the point." It is such a tired song; I roll my eyes, hoping no one sees. Our end of the table has gotten too quiet as she puts food on all the plates around her. Eyes turn to me, some embarrassed, some eager for a more brutal opinion. The uncle, once like a father to me, delivers.

"Well, I thought she'd come to her senses by now." He drops the words on top of my mumbled explanation of hijab, no one listening to what I didn't feel like saying anyway. His mouth twists into a frown, eyes darting my way from across the table as he goes on, louder, about people who forget where they came from, people who "pretend to be something they don't even understand."

"After all we been through with you, this is what you do? *Anything* for attention, I guess." It doesn't matter how true it is or not. When I'd first sat down, I'd planned to talk about the hectic final semester of my master's program and share the graduation photos for those who wanted to see. I'd printed them and put them in an album to be passed around. But even after the topic finally changes away from his remarks, I say nothing else and keep the album on my lap, not wanting anyone to notice it, each bite of food flavorless in my mouth.

I join in the after-meal cleanup, hoping to finally be allowed to speak on the fullness of my life now, without having to rehash old defenses. Mona and a few others keep each other company, gabbing about small things they assume I know nothing about as they put away food. It feels like too much to interfere. When I'm done at the sink, I had hoped to join their clique at the counter with their pie eating and giggles. Instead, they insist I go put my feet up; they'll do the rest. Mona's eyes cast a distance I'll never be able cross, not in a moment's time. It would be too obvious and too desperate to not do what I'm told.

I find my way upstairs to my old bedroom, now my mother's office, to take my time with the prayer I'm still learning. Halfway through my slow and warped Arabic, the door opens behind me, my mother sucks her teeth and curses though a rant meant to be heard by only me. I can't be sure if it's because of what I am doing or because I'm no longer welcome to roam the house, having tried so obviously to leave it and its ugly memories behind. Tears burn away my determination to make this work, to push away the demons that followed me here and the ones that sprang from the walls as soon as I'd walked in. The tears fall before I can try to send them back and pretend I'm not still hurt or afraid after all this time. I call for a cab before getting off my rug. The sight of my overnight bag is a joke, the punchline being how I ever thought I could come here and stuff away the damage, fake what we never had.

I take in more air hugs as I make my way out to the sound of a beeping horn, some going through the trouble to look sad. My mother stands with her hand on her hip in the doorway as I climb into the back seat, whatever she wanted to shout staying lodged in her throat. Sickeningly sweet relief and the feeling of having been rescued stay with me the whole three-hour ride back east.

Stepping into my tiny apartment, made fine with its second-hand treasures and my favorite colors, I exhale for what feels like the first time in a day. Jasmine leaps to her delicate paws, her sparkling eyes glad to see me. I hug her and prepare to collapse into bed. I wake up in full daylight, the evening before a dull and repeated nightmare that I don't need to dread anymore. I feel safe and at peace, my smile is easy and blessed. I take every call from the new friends who know about my fears and my struggle to rise above old troubles, who want to hear if it was as bad as I expected. I agree to meet up for coffee and real conversation, real laughter that leaves no one broken. I make a pact with myself that, moving forward, I will only agree to being seen as the whole person I've become, never mind what *was*. Later, when I'm alone again, I make lessons for the job I love, and work through my prayers with more diligence, intent on no longer worrying *who* will think *what* about me. I push harder to feel the soothing solidness of discovering and being myself in this place where I am free to exist on my own terms.

LOVE IN DARK TIMES
TEHMINA KHAN

At my parents' house in Milpitas after a lunch of Afghan food and masala dosas, my uncle, whom we call Moin Uncle, asks my parents to tell us their love story.

"Navaneeth Rao Uncle set them up," says Usmi, my sister. Dad's friend suggested him to Pappa, my grandfather, who was a chemistry professor at Osmania University in Hyderabad, India. As Dad was finishing his Ph.D., Pappa arranged for him to tutor Mom.

"But of course Mom didn't need tutoring!" we say. Mom has always been the sharpest one in the room, any room.

"But Laqa," says Moin Uncle, "after you married, Wajid Bhai came to the U.S., and you stayed back for six months to wait for your visa, and that must have been so terrible to be separated from each other. And the only way to communicate was by writing letters. I want to know… What did you say to each other in those letters?" Mom laughs a little. She's never been comfortable in the spotlight.

"The children are here," she says.

"There's only one child here," says Moin Uncle, looking at Omar, my fifteen-year-old son. My niece and nephew are off playing. But Mom stays silent. After all, her daughters are listening.

"So if Laqa won't tell us, Wajid Bhai, you must tell us. What did you tell each other in those letters?"

"In those days," Dad says, "it took ten days for a letter to reach its destination, then another ten days to receive a response. We would forget the details to which we were responding. Of course, then, we would write of romance… When, finally, I went to meet her at the airport, a couplet from Ghalib came to mind," and Dad recites in Urdu:

Wo ay hamare ghar khudha ki qudrat
kabhi ham unko dekhte hain kabhi wo hamko dekhte hain

She's come to me by the miracle of God
and all I can do is look at her as she looks at me.

"Wait, you said this to Mom?" I ask.

"Oh yes." My quiet understated dad, reciting poetry to my mom
– in the airport! Wow!

Moin Uncle then interrogates all of us. We hear how Saleem
Uncle serenaded Sogra Aunty at a medical school talent show. *Mere
mehboob aya hai…* He sings it for her still.

"Now, how about the younger generation?" Moin Uncle
continues, eyes shining. Charles looks at me. We've had a difficult year,
he and I, and I'm unwilling to speak first.

"She was late," he says, "and she's still always late." I tell
how I rushed to get in line for a sold-out movie at the San Francisco
International Film Festival, and he was right in front of me.

"What was this movie?"

"An Algerian movie, *Cheb* – about a young man who gets
deported from France to Algeria after committing a petty crime."

"We saw a different movie together," Charles tells them.

"We bought tickets for an added screening of *Cheb*," I say, "It
was a good movie."

Then Moin Uncle turns to Usmi and Juan, and Juan talks about
Usmi's first day of work at La Clinica de la Raza.

"She had an attitude," he says.

"Of course she did," I say. He tells us how a few months later,
in Ramadan, she was fasting and cranky.

"I went to ask her something and she cursed, and I thought,
I like her."

"But Moin Uncle, what about you?" we ask. Shammi Aunty
laughs and shakes her head.

"Okay, okay. I had a pediatrics exam coming up and went to
check out the textbook from the library. I got the book and was about
to leave, and I heard someone asking for the same book. The librarian
said, 'I'm sorry but he has taken the book, so you will need to wait until
it's returned.' Then I turned around and saw her and I said, 'Oh, you

need this book? How about you take it, but please promise me you will return it in four days.' 'I promise,' she said, and four days later, I got the book, and every few pages, there was a little note from her." Shammi Aunty rolls her eyes.

"So Omar, I want to ask you, which of these stories is the best one?" My son laughs but has no answer, and I tell them all a story from the Persian epic, *Shahnameh,* about how Manizheh, the Turkish princess, seduces Bizhan, a Persian warrior. They spend several blissful days together, but when he makes ready to go back to Persia, she slips something into his wine, takes him back to her palace and keeps him there as her kept man – until her father the king finds out, and trouble breaks out.

"That's pretty scary," says Omar.

It's an idyllic afternoon, sunlight streaming through the big windows, three generations laughing and telling love stories. Shammi Aunty and Moin Uncle are visiting from Memphis, Tennessee, and Sogra Aunty and Saleem Uncle are visiting from Trenton, New Jersey. They have voted already, and we are all enjoying the preciousness of each other's company.

That evening, Usmi and I both leave our parents' house with our husbands and kids to return to our respective homes in Albany and San Francisco, though three-year old Zahir stays back so six grandparents can lavish their attention on him. I spend the next two days getting out the vote for my county supervisor. My aunts, uncles and parents watch the election results together in Milpitas. As the electoral map turns red, I am too stunned and heartbroken to call them. *How is this possible?* The joyous conversation of Sunday seems a lifetime ago as the world we live in is plunged into a deep and painful darkness. My aunts and uncles go home to the task of protecting their communities. My parents, in immigrant-rich Silicon Valley, worry and wait. And I, in San Francisco, where our progressive-moderate rivalry comes to a halt, weep for the country, and brace myself for the rash of hate crimes.

Our family has been here for fifty years. My aunts and uncles are doctors; my parents are scientists. They have established mosques and cultural communities and have spent sleepless nights anguishing over their children's future in this new place. We have grown roots here and have made a home for ourselves with our hands and with our stories. And yet, the resentment from the middle of the country has spoken, and it is a resentment against us – for being Muslim, brown, and immigrant, but also for being educated and worldly. Poor white people go to the hospital to get treated by wealthy brown doctors with accents, who speak in complete sentences. Their country is changing – and here is their whitelash against us. After Obama, they elect an openly bigoted and misogynist candidate for their president. He says he will build a wall. He says he will carry out a mass deportation. He says he will create a registry of Muslims. He brags about sexual assault. *He* says he is not my president, and so I will take him at his word until he proves otherwise.

The next shell-shocked morning, we return to the task of education. Omar goes to school, and we go to City College, where Charles teaches math and I teach writing. My colleagues choke back tears. I see fear in my students' eyes. Who will be deported? Who will be harassed? Whose lives matter now? Our students are from everywhere, speak many languages, and they come here to open their minds, to think critically, and to solve problems so they may develop a career, make a decent living, and more importantly, so they may shape our world. This is why I teach writing – to help my students claim a voice and participate in public discourse. In class, we discuss the urgency of speaking out. We tell them that San Francisco is a sanctuary city, that we as a city will protect them. We talk about taking care of each other. And yet we struggle to hold back the fear we wear on our faces. We know it will not be okay, and we won't lie to our students.

Omar and his classmates walk from school to Civic Center and join with over a thousand high school students to defend their humanity and their right to exist. Last week their theater department performed *The Diary of Anne Frank,* and we can't help but wonder, *Is this happening now?*

At the oldest farmers' market in the city, Grace, the Japanese-American farmer from the valley, is packing up early because Leora, her assistant, who years ago painted murals on Omar's preschool vans, is attending Muhammad's daughter's henna party in Sacramento. Muhammad is a quiet Pakistani farmer who sells persimmons and pomegranates this time of year, whose younger son is Omar's age. I tell Leora about my own henna party twenty years ago, and suggest she caffeinate herself for a long night. Nash, the Palestinian olive grower who taught me how to cure olives, tells me things will turn out okay. We've been through bad times before. He'll have the manzanillo olives next week, he says, unless it rains. At Sukhi's Indian food stall, the Afghan employee talks to two customers in Spanish, explaining what a samosa is. I join in and he tells me my Spanish is good. I tell him the same, and we laugh. "*Khudhahafiz Tehmina jan*," he says. An endearment from a stranger. I like that.

I return to my two-block street in Bernal Heights, sit in my parked car, and look at my neighbors' houses. Some of us have been here for three generations, and some have just arrived. Here, educators, nurses, nuns, construction workers, electricians, software engineers, and artists all coexist. We are Muslim, Jewish, Catholic, Protestant, Jehovah's Witness, Hindu, Buddhist, and agnostic. We are Latino, African American, Asian and European. Some of us arrived without papers and worked multiple jobs to make a home here. Our kids live with single moms, single dads, two moms, two dads, grandparents, and moms and dads. Some have special needs. One is a stellar musician. We have survived eviction attempts, violence, and vandalism. We reach our hands out to Anna whose wife Carla died of cancer, and we seek justice for Alex, who was murdered by a police officer two years ago. Of course we have our differences, mostly around who's blocking whose driveway, but we greet each other by name and smile. Morgan, a trans woman who used to be an iron worker in New Jersey, pulls up on her scooter.

"I need to build something," she says.

"Can you build a wall around California?" I ask, and we talk about keeping the almonds and iPhones to ourselves.

Two weeks later we celebrate Thanksgiving with another side of my family, and we suspend our public grief for a private one. Outside, by candlelight, we remember Helen, my feisty Filipina-Salvadoran, native San Franciscan mother-in-law who died one year ago on Thanksgiving Day. Kai, my African-American father-in-law is recovering from surgery but still serenades her memory on the saxophone of his mind. *The ideal American* is how a friend once described Charles. And so we give thanks in an ideal America – a family that began when a Filipino laborer asked a Salvadoran domestic worker to dance – a family that is ever opening its arms. We are Catholic, Protestant, Jewish, Buddhist, and Muslim. Our skin tones range from espresso to cream. African-American Jalen has two white moms; Maya and Zoe's dad speaks to them in Russian; little Alessandra will travel to Peru with a dozen family members to visit her grandparents; teenage Alanis brings the Philippines back to us; and my tall teenage Omar speaks fluent Spanish and cooks Indian fusion food. We serve up dal, Peruvian potatoes, chicken adobo, and mac and cheese, along with the turkey. And we tell more love stories. We tell stories because our lives depend on them. Each story connects with other stories and keeps us human in an inhumane time. We tell stories, knowing that only our collective humanity will carry us through the darkness.

And so I give thanks for *this* America – the America of jazz, Mexican ballads, Chinese opera, and Urdu love songs; the America of bok choy, daikon radish, persimmons and chili peppers; the America that is constantly teaching me new words and new dance moves; the America that welcomes me and loves me, and that I, too, love. And this America would not exist but for the blood, sweat, and tears of so many who came before us. And so even as I give thanks, I stand ready to defend this precious home we keep on building one love story at a time.

PART FOUR:
BLOOD
HARMONIES

WORDS FOR A DISTANT GRANDFATHER
TEHMINA KHAN

Your pen.
The cracked grey casing held together
with black tape.
(I broke it when I dropped it after signing a check.)

In California,
I hold this Parker fountain pen.
Ink flows into journeys
as you discovered so many years ago.

How many hypotheses, equations, and results?
How many stories and letters passed through this pen?
How can one person know so much?
Patience and hard work, you say without words.
Hours become days.
Days become years.
Everything we learn adds up.

In Hyderabad,
I sit with you.
Your hands tremble.
Your black-framed glasses slide down your nose.
I adjust them so you can read the Urdu newspaper,
the one that calligraphers still scribe by hand
in a dusty office somewhere
in Hyderabad.

You speak to me in your proper Oxford English
even though I have learned to speak Urdu,
but your words hesitate, as if to search for their sound.
You breathe.

Each word is a trembling whisper
between gasps for air.

In Hyderabad,
it is dinnertime and I feed you soft rice with a spoon.

In Ireland,
you hold the spoon.
You say "*khana kao*" and you put soft *kichari* in my mouth.
"*Kao,*" I repeat.
My young parents look up and carve this moment
in the craggy stones of their temporary home.
kao
eat —
a word!

In California,
you talk to me in big words,
not like the grandfathers in storybooks who like to joke and tickle.

You tell me about Claudius
and give me a yellow field guide
full of tiger swallowtails, monarchs, katydids, and dragonflies.
When you see me reading, you always walk softly
and turn on an extra light.

In Hyderabad,
we bring you a wheelchair,
so you can come out of your room,
but you grasp at the walker instead,
while your attendant supports you from behind.
Each step a jagged stone
tumbling forward.

You come to the living room
to watch the documentary I made about the Palestinians.
You smile a smile of sorrow.
I don't know if you understand,
but your eyes shine
as they did when you taught me to play chess
eighteen years ago in California.
A quiet laugh escapes.

In California,
you walk home from the grocery store
while the rest of us ride in the car.
You need to walk, you say.

Now,
In California,
I understand.

In Hyderabad,
I want to photograph you in black and white
as you read the Urdu paper,
your black framed glasses sliding down your nose,
you in your empty room with just a bed, a chair and an armoire.
(You have donated your books to the library.)
Your sagging face gazing.
Your name plate "Prof. S.S. Muhammad"
sitting alone on an empty shelf.

But I don't think you want to be photographed,
so I keep the camera in my bag
and hold onto the picture in my mind.

In California,
I write with your pen,
then place the papers
in the leather portfolio patched with black tape
that you kept at your pillow
in Hyderabad,
filled with photographs and letters
and my poems which Mom sent you.

In Hyderabad,
your eyes follow me and Usmi
as we leave to board a train to see our uncles.
Will we leave for America without returning to you?
You ask without words.

No,
but you can see our departure coming.
After we return to you,
the airline calls to tell us our flight is leaving one day early.
We pack our suitcases and hug you quickly.
Your glazed eyes follow us as we run out the door.

I see you now
four and a half feet tall,
your toothless face sagging,
your joints tied up in knots,
yet you shine with a grace I do not understand.

I see you long ago and I wonder,
Is time an enemy or a friend?

In Hyderabad,
Ammam returns home from the airport
and finds you crying.
"This was our last encounter," you tell her.

In California,
Mom boards a plane to Hyderabad
and we read Qur'an
and pray for your safe journey
to where we all return.

In California,
I hold onto an echo of your soft voice.
I grasp your grey Parker fountain pen
and link myself to your grasp
of words
which linger
for me
and those who will follow.

OF MOLTEN CHOCOLATE CAKES AND MOTHERS
BARAA ARAR

Molten chocolate cakes are my mother's favourite dessert. I mean, maybe they are not her *absolute* favourite, but if she had a list of top ten, they'd be up there. I remember vividly one night when she came home from one literary event or another and gushed about these little warm chocolate pots with a creamy center that she devoured. The following Mother's Day, I woke up earlier than the rest of the family and made them for us. I served them with whipped cream and fresh fruit. They turned out delicious. Until this day, my first try at that dessert was my best try. I made them a few times since, but never to the same calibre of success.

Being in the kitchen was part of my childhood. I grew up surrounded by two very strong women—my mother and her mother. And there was always one place where those women co-existed—the kitchen. I grew up learning how to cook by watching my grandma move effortlessly from the counter to the sink to the stovetop. Upon my return from school, I would throw my bag onto the couch, run into the kitchen, and see what I could do to help my grandmother. Most of the time I was assigned the most mundane tasks, the tasks she didn't want to do. So I would peel the sticky skin off the grilled peppers. I would chop the onions behind a screen of tears.

My grandmother cooked every day. Sometimes it felt like she spent the whole day cooking. For Eid, the festive preparations stretched over a few days. She would roll out dough for fresh *nawsr*, a semolina-based Tunisian noodle. She rolled and dyed marzipan to make *ka'ber*, colourful almond sweets coated in granulated sugar. All our plastic containers and empty yogurt tubs were full of some sort of delicacy. As a child, I didn't grasp the effort exuded in this culinary enterprise. It took me a while to learn that good, proper Tunisian food, comfort food that is, took hours of slow relentless simmering. Tunisian dishes, like most home cooking, are the product of long, patient hours. They are product of women who spend much of their day at home, toiling away for their families, or for those who can afford it, a hired cook to replace them.

As a teenager, I stopped giving my grandmother a hand in the kitchen. I hoarded my free labour because I was too busy having friends, or eating Dairy Queen at the beach, or hanging out on the periphery of my high school's yard. I was too busy and too cool to help my own grandmother. Such is teenage-hood. But every once in a while, I would throw myself back into the kitchen for isolated occasions. With an upbringing steeped in the kitchen, I did not shy away from pancake breakfasts, potluck dinners, or school bake sales.

The kitchen is a mass producer of comfort and goodness: birthday cake, anniversary dinners, Mother's Day brunch. But kitchens also incubate disasters. Burns. Scratches. Cuts. Salting something instead of adding sugar. Disasters are natural outcomes of kitchen experimentation. And experiments breed arguments. Whenever I helped my grandmother peel the grilled peppers or chop the onions, she would inevitably have something to say about my technique. There would always be a snide word about how young girls these days did a subpar job in the kitchen. One time during high school, my grandmother softly coerced me into the kitchen to teach me how to de-bone a chicken. I was seventeen and interested in boys and my skinny jeans and getting into university. I was interested in lots of things. Deboning a chicken was not one of them. In typical teenage fashion, I initially refused. But that was not an option for her. My grandmother literally dragged me into the kitchen, put a knife in my hand, and made me find the breast tendon and make an incision. I remember crying as I looked for the bone with my pointer finger, thinking to myself, "None of my white friends have to engage in such backwards traditions." But like with everything, it was over shortly after it started, and I went back to thinking about boys and skinny jeans and getting into university.

Familial relationships thrive in the kitchen, despite failed experiments. It is no coincidence an IKEA advertisement titled "Nonna" is built on the premise of an unimpressionable Italian matriarch, whose silent stamp of approval causes her family members to walk on eggshells. The ad captures the impossibly awkward power dynamics that underlie how we interact with our families. Those petty and mundane arguments shape our relationships. Kitchens create delicious meals and wreak havoc. Kitchens are where we keep the knives. Kitchen are where the pans are scalding and the tempers are hot. And yet, after a long day, we find ourselves back in the kitchen, cooking for our families or making ourselves a cup of tea.

No matter how much I wanted to hide away in my room from my weird immigrant family and deboning chickens and home cooking, they stubbornly crept back into my life. Now that I am a little less angry with my world, I love hosting a large *iftar* every Ramadan. I invite my friends, friends of friends, siblings of friends, and we break our fasts together. I love hosting people in my home during Ramadan. While the rest of the neighbourhood gets ready to rest their eyes at 9:45 p.m., my Muslim friends, and some non-Muslims who tag along, flock to my place to gorge on stuffed dates, lentil soup, lamb stew, grilled peaches. In a world plagued with inequality and confusion, the simple act of eating together in the late hours, among second generation Muslims, is therapeutic. I do not have to cook. I live at home, with plenty of established and inspiring cooks ready to whip something up for me. But I like to cook. I cook to remember. I cook to forget. To make something. To feel useful. I write for the same reasons.

Right now, I am writing because I failed to make good molten chocolate cakes. Again. I forgot to add the flour and there was not nearly enough sugar to thicken the eggy mixture. So my family had to endure subpar molten chocolate cakes. In the grand scheme of things, chocolate is chocolate. I still felt bad about it. As I made the dessert, my mom came to help. She asked if I should use a whisk instead of a spatula, and I retorted back self-assuredly: "You don't trust me!" I regressed back into that seventeen-year-old girl unwillingly deboning a chicken.

My sharp words send us into a bickering match. I tell her it is about trusting my skills. She tells me this is not about trust. We are both spitting images of our own mothers. We go back and forth, like clockwork. We play a game of tug of war, with two equally strong, independent, female contestants. Sometimes she slips and I win, but only momentarily, until I slip and she takes up her triumphal maternal place.

My relationship with my mother, grandmother, and food is complicated. Being in the kitchen taught me that day-to-day life is not always easy, at least not for my integrational, immigrant family. On TV, white families always looked so happy. They had movie nights and taco Tuesdays, and the white moms never seemed to be cross with their kids. At our house, we always seemed to bicker about nothing and everything all the time. Our issues were compounded and amplified by cultural miscommunications, intergenerational divides, and always in the background, was the inherently fragmented diaspora experience. We argued. But food made it better. Food always made it better.

Sometimes I resented my family for making so much of our life about food. In high school, I heard a rumour that the stepmother of one of the senior girls, one of the skinny blond white ones, locks the pantry so the girls don't snack. I heard she forces them to have salad for at least one meal a day. A part of me thought this is psychopathic, but another part of me felt envious. If my family controlled my eating that way, maybe I would not be as chubby in the middle. A part of me was angry all sorts of delicious food was readily accessible for consumption at our house. We were always thinking about what next to cook, what we need to defrost so we can prepare the next meal. There was always something to be said about food.

Whenever my friends came over I had to explain to them what we were eating for dinner. "It's like Tunisian pasta," I would say. I tried to provide them a reference point, to make the foreign relatable to their upper-middle-class white experiences. Their parents would pick them up after a night of eating and studying and thank my mom for "feeding my kid." My mom never understood that gratitude; these were the rules of hospitability in our culture—if someone comes over, naturally, you feed them.

My grandmother feels important in the kitchen. Her family circumstances dictated she grew up with limited formal education and a young marriage. She always prides herself on being a wonderful cook. But of course, my grandmother had to learn somewhere. She was someone's daughter. She served her time dutifully chopping onions and peeling grilled peppers. By the time she was nineteen, she was ready to wed and knew the quintessential Tunisian dishes. "I knew nothing when I got married," her narrative arc begins. But now, she is our matriarchal cook. Even when she goes home to Tunisia, her family members beg her to make their favourites. The comfort food classics. Couscous with lamb. *Shakshuka* (poached eggs in spiced sauce) with *merguez* (sausage). *Breek* (Tunisian springrolls). The childhood dishes they crave but can't make quite right themselves.

My mother, Tunisian-born, came to Canada in her early twenties for her graduate studies. She brought with her a working knowledge of Tunisian dishes, but inevitably, like many immigrants, she adopted a hybrid kitchen experience. So my mom grills salmon and bakes banana bread and cooks couscous the white way (to my grandmother's horror). Food is a vehicle for cultural transfer of knowledge. In my mother's life, the kinds of food she makes are markers of integration and change. My Tunisian grandmother's own culinary evolution continued, no matter how much she contested it. She learned to make Tandoori and butter chicken from her Indian friends, recipes with their own unique colonial history. But my grandmother doesn't know that; good food is good food.

Our family's fixation used to anger me. Why did we have to eat differently from others? Why was our food so fatty? So saucy? So much? Among many other aspects, my family's approach to food marked us as different from the dominant culture. As a teenager, this made me resentful. As the children of immigrants, much of our early life revolves around experimentation, not only in the kitchen, but in a system rigged against people who look like us. Who pray like us. Who eat like us. It took me a long time to understand why my grandmother spent so much of her day cooking. In the moments of inevitable confusion and uncertainty, in the moments of intense *dépaysement*, cooking meals from "back home" is a great solace. I now understand this almost compulsive need to cook. We cook to remember. We cook to forget. We cook to make something. We cook to feel useful. We write for the same reasons.

MY FATHER
@STUDENTASIM

Over half a century ago, in 1965, my father came to Canada as a student from Pakistan. He was twenty-eight. He was accepted to Queen's University in Kingston, Ontario, where he went on to complete a Master of Science in Mathematics degree.

"The secret of life is to read," my father told me one day. My father had to literally read to give me and my family opportunity. He was called "*Ghut wala chacha.*" *Ghut* means corner in Punjabi. My father's family tells me how Dad used to sprinkle turmeric around himself as he would sit and study on the floor in the famous corner of their home. This way, ants would not come around and bite him, and he could submerge himself in his books and studies without fear!

He was dedicated. After he failed grade eight, he changed his mindset and never looked back. He came in second at Punjab University in his M.Sc. Mathematics degree in his graduating year.

Leaving Pakistan was no small feat. One day, he got wind of "Queen's University" from a colleague who did not want to share any information about this Canadian learning institution, probably thinking Dad would be competition for him. Despite this, Dad learned the name. What he did next was nothing short of remarkable. He wrote a letter requesting admission.

To: Queen's University, Canada.

This is all he wrote for the address. No city, no further address. It still amazes me to this day. And as they say, the rest is history. Miraculously, Queen's responded with a letter of acceptance and a plane ticket a few months later. Utterly surprised, Dad prepared to come to Canada.

In 1965, leaving Pakistan for a foreign country was like entering into an abyss. What would happen after, nobody knew. There was no detailed information about settling in foreign countries, no internet, no instant communication methods, and even telephones were scarce. Besides, most fellow countrymen that did leave headed for the UK, not Canada.

Relatives were concerned because they wondered if they would ever see their loved ones again. My *dadi*, my grandmother (my father's mother), was so afraid for him that she did not want him to leave. Dad insisted and he tells me the day he left, Dadi tied verses of the Qur'an to his arm for protection.

Living in Canada back in those days was truly an act of courage and resilience. Being an immigrant, a minority, a Muslim, being different, an other, and living without any family, with no financial security, and in a land that knew little about foreigners, is something hard to imagine. How did he make it? I wonder sometimes, if I was in his shoes, could I have done the same?

My father in one word: Consistent. He has always had routine, always had structure. Knowing him, I can describe him as a good man, a hardworking man, an honest man, and a man who "doesn't want to bother anybody."

Indeed Dad worked hard. He wanted to succeed. And by the will of Allah, he did. Recently, I developed an artistic concept called *The Champion for Life*™. A Champion for Life™ is someone who honours themselves "for life" and recognizes there is always a consistent Process, in order to make Progress. It is a life endeavour. My father embodies this process; I have witnessed his consistency. He gets up every day at that same time, early morning before sun-up, even on weekends, reads Qur'an, stretches, eats breakfast and then goes for a walk. And I have seen this not just some times, but all the time, throughout the decades. The Process creates champions; the Process is the cure for challenges. I have never seen this man deviate from his Process nor his work. My father is A Champion for Life™.

In 2016, I had the opportunity of a lifetime to tell his story when I produced *The Champion for Life*™ film. It was filmed on location, where it all started, in Dad's home city of Faisalabad, Pakistan. Since exploring the arts, I have been fortunate enough to place the teachings of my parents in my work in various ways. This film project was no different, but this time, I *directly* incorporated Dad's story into my own. The film was a bridge between Dad, myself and the future.

We filmed on our last day before leaving Pakistan, gathering the raw materials literally the night before, obtaining police permission to shoot, and acquiring the services of a film crew I had never met, who had zero advance film direction, not knowing if they would really arrive. Everything unfolded the moment we met. The way the film came together was purely a miracle.

I owe my father too much and I am forever indebted. I am thankful to Allah for granting me such an example. Indeed he is an angel in my life. I pray that Allah protects my father always. And I pray that I can become some of the man that my father will always be.

BLOOD HARMONIES
FAISAL MOHYUDDIN

To remember my mother crouching in our kitchen,
putting into place a new floor of ceramic tiles,
is to remember her blood hopes, her effervescent hunger
to keep the feet of her five kids from slipping
into the wrong kind of slide. Stay one with one another,
in blood harmony, she would say, meaning
brother and sister, Muslim and Muslim, blood and blood.
Pointing down at the tiles, she would say,
Look how the pattern comes together,
forms a larger mosaic of meaning. You should live like this.
Most of the time, I nodded my head, not knowing
how else to respond, agreeing because it was simpler.
But sometimes, standing there, looking down
at a floor not yet finished, at naked patches revealing
a history of vinyl, broken and stained, I would think,
I just can't be happy living so small, so safe.
Then I would see, in those unfinished places, the face
of some girl I had met the other day,
whose name I never asked, knowing it was pointless.
I would stand there in the kitchen, thinking
how badly I wanted to know that girl's name, to believe in it
like a new religion, like my own blood,
how I wanted to let myself fall in love with her,
because that girl had smiled at me, because that girl was real
and alive, not like one of those phantom wives
my mother saw in her dreams and spoke of in metaphors.

STOP BEING SO PICKY, OR WHY I DIDN'T MARRY MY CAT
KATIE MIRANDA AL ALI

Your married friends, your parents, your grandparents are all telling you to stop being so picky and settle down and get married.

God knows your parents didn't face the dating challenges you are: the swiping, the ghosting, the cute guy/girl who turns out to not look at all like their picture, the "u r hot, what r u doing" messages...

They tell you to stop being so picky. But what does that mean? Does it mean "settling?" No, not at all. It means expanding your horizons and letting go of limiting beliefs. Here's an example of what that meant for me.

So, there I was in 2015, a 40-year-old Muslim woman and the ink just drying on my divorce paperwork. "Doomed to a life of a cat lady spinster" was the expression I saw on other Muslims' faces when I told them my age and marital status.

Since I'm a convert, they knew I didn't have Muslim parents who would "find me a good husband."

But I wasn't giving up. After my divorce, now I finally knew what I wanted and DIDN'T want, right? I made a list of primary qualities: He has to: 1) be cute, 2) be Muslim, 3) be financially stable, 4) lead a healthy lifestyle, and 5) have no children living with him.

Tall order, you say, for a 40-year old divorcée? The thing is, these were non-negotiable for me.

1) I had to be attracted to him.

2) Since I am Muslim, I wanted to meet someone who would fast Ramadan with me, go on the hajj pilgrimage with me and do the daily prayers together with me. It was a matter of sharing the same values and being on the same page, and I couldn't get that with a non-Muslim.

3) My ex-husband was dependent on me financially, and this caused
a lot of problems in the marriage. I knew I didn't want to go through that again.

4) What this meant to me is that I couldn't live with a couch potato or someone who smoked or drank, and I met many Muslims who did both! I'm active and healthy and I wanted someone who was also. Plus, it would make life together more fun.

5) I did not want to live with someone else's kids or to be put in a stepmother role. Not that there is anything wrong with that. It just wasn't
for me.

These things weren't "checklist items" for me. They reflected the values and character traits that I wanted to find in the man of my dreams – a man who was spiritual, trustworthy, responsible, and ambitious. I wanted to share my life with a man I could trust and who inspired me.

Oh! I also had a list of secondary qualities, one of which, in my head, was a primary quality:

6) He has to have been born or, at least, raised in the U.S.

You see, my ex-husband was not born and raised in the U.S., and I believed that one of the primary reasons for our divorce was the "clash of cultures" myth. I was dead set on never considering anyone who hadn't been in the U.S. for at least their teenage years. And no Saudis. Definitely, no Saudis! I have a girlfriend who was married to a Saudi and the horror stories she told... Wow! Can't have any guy telling me I have to wear a hijab or that I can't drive a car, right?

By the time 2016 rolled around, I had met and chatted with quite a few men over various Muslim and non-Muslim apps and sites. No one was a good fit. I was racking up quite a collection of my own horror stories.

And then on Twitter of all places, a guy DM'd me after I posted a photo of a café in Portland I had been to that day. He said he had also been there that day, but we had not seen each other. We chatted a little and then he asked me out for coffee. I looked at his profile and it said he lived in Qatif and Portland. I didn't know where Qatif was, but I took a guess it was in Saudi Arabia, and sure enough it was. No, not a Saudi! Too bad, 'cuz he was cute! And it seemed we had a lot of shared interests judging by his Twitter timeline. That's the thing with Twitter; you can get a pretty good idea of what the person is actually into. He was into hiking, nature, Bernie Sanders, cats, and women's rights, just like me! Hmm, not exactly my stereotype of a Saudi.

I cautiously agreed to go out for coffee.

Fast forward four years and we are married and just welcomed a son. He is everything on my primary list and more.

If I had nixed him because of my prejudices about Saudis (I'd only ever met one Saudi before him by the way), I would have nixed the love of my life. When I saw 35-year-old Muslim men limiting themselves to women age 18-30 in their profiles, it made me wonder who they might be missing out on. There was one guy on Minder who was five years younger than me and who texted me, "you're pretty, too bad you're too old for me." Yeah, too bad for him. My husband is five years younger than me btw.

When I hear women saying, "Well, he has to be a Punjabi Pakistani like me," or "He can't be Shia," or "He has to make a certain amount of money per year," or "He has to be at least six feet tall," I wonder what kind of amazing guys they might be missing out on. What if the man of your dreams makes $5,000 less a year than your requirement, or is 5'11" instead of 6'?

Are you willing to miss out on the love of your life based on some numbers?

These are ego-based desires, not value-based desires. Just like my desire to meet and marry a man who was raised in the U.S.

One last piece of advice, while Twitter is not a dating platform, it has one advantage that other sites and apps don't: you can truly learn a lot about someone and their actual interests by reading their timeline. Are they an argumentative asshole on Twitter? If so, it's pretty easy to tell and pass them over. Are they respectful even when they disagree with someone, or do they name call? If they name call on Twitter, they're probably going to do that to you, too.

Good luck to all the singles out there. I know how hard it is. But if you truly believe you will find your match and let go of limiting beliefs about what that person has to be, you will.

LUNCH HOUR
SHEREEN HUSSAIN

My journey to America began over thirty years ago on a British Airways flight from Heathrow. I was fresh out of college, armed with a spirit of optimism for my new American life and a notebook full of hand-written recipes for Hyderabadi cuisine. Phone calls to my mother were misty-eyed sessions once a week if our budget allowed. Checking the mailbox for letters from home became an hourly obsession.

But my husband was a good, kind soul, and as we got acquainted, I began to wish we could spend more time together. He worked long hours in a skyscraper about a block away from Market Street in San Francisco. This street was home to stores with large picture windows showcasing sumptuous designer clothes draped on moody mannequins. Tucked in between these was one of the last remaining Woolworth's** in the state of California. I was still acclimatizing myself from moving to England. I had not started work yet and was still adjusting to time zones, the language and the considerable cultural differences. For instance, office lunches in Europe are often elaborate affairs. People really take the time to have a complete break from work, and are just a tad bit less driven.

One day, I thought I would surprise my new mate by taking him out to a restaurant near his office. The number 21 bus went from Hayes Street near our apartment on Stanyan all the way downtown. I donned a frilly, magenta English dress and called him from a payphone on Market, laughing at my own excitement.

He could not meet me for lunch.

He apologized, told me I should grab a bite to eat and explore the city. I was crestfallen and thought he was just being hermit-like, unable to let go of his bachelor lifestyle. Years later, I was to discover that in the U.S., many companies don't really have such a thing as a lunch hour. Lunch in the U.S. may be an un-ceremonial twenty-minute sandwich eaten at a desk in a cubicle.

The walls of the payphone booth seemed to be closing in on me like a scene from a Stephen King novel. Everything around me felt hostile. What was I thinking?

I was married to a man I hardly knew. San Francisco had the ocean and valleys and eternal sunshine, but I had left behind my precious family, and my beloved England. I was friendless and was in a textbook arranged marriage. I leaned against the Nordstrom pillars and looked across the street. I knew I should just take the number 21 home again, make myself a cheese sandwich, do some dusting and start preparing a lamb curry for the evening dinner.

In the meantime, I wandered around Market Street, enquiring where the bus stop was, but people were either too busy or did not understand my accent.

Then I spied a sign: Woolworth and Company.

I almost fainted. There had been an F.W. Woolworth on Plumstead High Street where I grew up. Too many memories to count. I would tag along with my mother for some mundane kitchen-related purchase, hoping for a bar of chocolate as a reward. It had served as a central meeting point for shopping trips with my two best friends from high school, Carol Durrant and Sandra Smythe. These were giddy, giggly girly outings stretching out our weekly £1.50 allowance.

That settled it. I entered the seedy yet thriving establishment and saw that they had a small lunch counter. Their sandwiches were within reach of me, the fiscally cautious new bride and child of immigrants.

I ordered tuna and asked for take away. This is where the problem began.

"You want what, honey?"

"Take away," I responded raising my voice.

"You want to take what away?" replied the puzzled sandwich server, smoothing down her pink uniform.

I needed to be more specific. "I want to take the food away from here and eat it somewhere else," came my information-packed explanation.

Light dawned. "Oh, I get it!" burst out the server. "You want the sandwich to go." To go. So that was how I wanted it. I had to repeat the phrase to myself daily like a new *surah*. That marked the beginning of a twenty-year stint of trying to be understood in my adopted country.

Nappies would become diapers, petrol was gas, sheddule was skedule. There was no greengrocer, just a large store where one bought pro-DOOS. Pancakes were not wafer thin crepes upon which one sprinkled powdered sugar and lemon juice; they were thick, round creations bearing lashings of maple syrup. I could not find a single sitcom even mildly amusing for at least fifteen years, when I slowly began to understand the humour and started spelling it "humor." After that, I finally had to let go of the view that I was better than everyone else around me.

Yet, as low as I felt that day, I was not desperate enough to eat my lunch inside the rundown store. There was a small square where old men played chess and young buskers collected pennies by singing Beatles songs. Next to them, tourists lined up to catch a festive cable car for a day of sightseeing. I believed I could become invisible here and found a spot next to a person in dusty pants who requested some spare change. I obliged, then gave him a piece of my tuna sub, and he melted away into the crowd.

"There are places I remember all my life…" sang the spirited musician, and a tear fell into my sandwich creating a small, damp patch on the bread. I was ready to feel extremely sorry for myself. Being amongst all these homeless people should have ended my self-indulgence fest, but it simply made me feel even sadder. Just then I heard a loud clanging sound. A cable car. The elderly driver of this magnificent vehicle looked straight over at me, adjusting his cap. "You need to get on board and go look at the ocean," he said. This driver's knowledge was not limited to timetables and cable tracks. He had a point.

I needed to turn the loneliness into freedom, an opportunity to explore. This could be a new beginning for me. A new city, a new life. I could get a graduate degree, read all the books on the endless lists I had compiled, start crocheting again, become a domestic goddess or maybe even a writer? Did I really just want to be the full-time wife, pining at home in a tiny apartment for the husband who worked ten hour days?

As I dug around in my purse for the necessary cable car fare, I spied someone out of the corner of my eye, running towards me. I had been warned about muggings, shootings and general urban crime by my husband. His exact words had been, "You're not in safe old Plumstead Common anymore." I zipped up my handbag, pulled it close to me and looked up.

The aforementioned spouse was standing in front of me, panting from running so hard.

"Sorry for not being able to have lunch with you," he said between breaths. "I felt so terrible I took the rest of the day off. It's just that we only get half an hour and by the time… well, anyway, where do you want to eat? There is a lovely French bakery I've been wanting to take you to. Next to that awful Woolworth's place."

Had he really taken the day off for me? This was America, where you were only allocated a meager ten whole vacation days a year.

"Oh, Woolworth's isn't so bad," I responded, taking his hand.

* Editor's Note: Woolworth closed its last remaining stores in 1997, bringing an end to this iconic San Francisco landmark and an end to the dime store era.

JASMINE
REEM HAMMAD

It is Jasmine I smell. The scent that brings memories to mind.

Jasmine. Every morning, my grandmother picked new buds from the bushes surrounding her house and sprinkled them in bunches inside her linen closet. It was her ritual. The new buds would pour their perfume, wilt, die and be transformed.

When I was a little girl, staying over at my grandmother's house, I would watch her arrange her freshly scented, crisply folded whites in that closet. What always attracted my attention were her bath towels. They were large and plenty. The kind that covered you from head to toe like a shroud. They were white and had fringes all around their sides. Some had an added gold embroidered design, a design that was fit to be seen and admired, most probably by the ladies in the *hamams* (public baths) bathing side by side with my grandmother.

I looked forward during my bath to the moment when my grandmother would hand me one of her prized towels to wrap my toasty, steamy, freshly scrubbed body. I would grab the towel with great excitement to quickly contain the heat escaping the surface of my skin. The towel, wrapped around me, became alive again. Flowery smells were revived by the steam and humidity. Feelings of gratitude and delight would overwhelm and humble me at once.

I would often wait a while, covered with my white bath attire, to rest my tired body and for my temperature to normalize. As I would begin to put my clothes on, little butterfly-like creatures pressed against my skin would come flying out in the air and slowly fall to the ground. Startled at first, I would step back to examine the creatures closely. They were lifeless and seemed to take on a different posture lying on the Persian-carpeted floor. After picking one up, I finally determined their identity. They were the jasmine my grandmother had picked earlier in the week, carefully placed in her linen closet, passionately tucked in between her sheets and towels.

Jasmine. The smell makes me long to be with her, to be tickled by the butterflies that blessed my bed sheets, and the flowers that filled my nightly dreams.

HOW CAN TWO HEARTS FULLY CONNECT IF THEY DON'T SPEAK THE SAME? • KHADIJO ABDI

In between the time they are out of school and before they go to sleep, you are constantly reminding them of how many ways you were different from them when you were their age. Every chance, when you have them in the car, you tell how much better you treated your parents. In fact, it is your favorite time to do it when you have them as captives. "My mother never had to tell me," you like to say. "Just one look and I knew what she wanted to be done. Back home people show respect for their parents," you lament.

But you fail to see that those latest model gadgets that harvest their attention, those same gadgets you put in their hands to bribe them into doing things and to keep them occupied, took their eyes away from you. You can give them all the looks you've got, but they will not lift their heads from the screens long enough to see it. You were too busy to spend time with them, or you didn't want them running in your well-set living room, and you didn't feel they were safe outside with those kids you fear will give them a taste for illicit things, or even worse, introduce them to feeling comfortable with the opposite gender and mingling freely. You would rather they sit quietly, and the screens let them do that. You let them keep the electronics even though you fear them posting grinning pictures on social media, their arms wrapped around girls from school. You worry about him, your little boy who spent so many Sundays in advanced *tahfiid* class, even though you never taught him the meaning of the Qur'an recited so beautifully.

You worry how much time your daughter spends, her ears plugged, staring at screens, her head hunched over like she carries the weight of the world. You used to keep them busy when they were younger with Islamic studies and math tutoring. But now their grades in school mean everything. You want them getting top marks, their GPA the highest among their peers. You pay extra for those practice tests so they may go sit in a stuffy room on a particular Saturday, with a no. 2 pencil in hand and a sheet of pink in front of them, so they can supply the right answers to questions they will never encounter in real life. Even if they were sick that Saturday morning, sniffling and stuffy-nosed, you would still fill their bellies with tart orange juice, the cheap kind that lasts forever in the fridge, and drive them to a random suburb, you and them alone on the road, because it is a Saturday morning, and everyone is resting their weary bodies. You do all of this hoping they get into the best schools, hoping their grades can pay the bill for their studies, so they may become doctors or engineers. Never mind that your boy is too faint-hearted for the cadavers in medical school and squeamish over any diseased body fluid or phlegmy cough. Or that math bores him to tears, so engineering will slowly suffocate his soul.

And your daughter would rather be a poet or social organizer; she is not sure which one yet. She is only fourteen. You are pushing her towards becoming a doctor, or at the very least, a nurse or a teacher. You question her choices. "What could you possibly do with poetry?" And you cajole her, "Become a doctor, become a teacher, become a nurse, and you could live anywhere and make a decent life." You say this even though you don't really mean anywhere; you were picturing her back home in your city, in your village. You say it to her even though you know that this is her home. She has spent all her time right here. Those nostalgic feelings you have about back home are not hers. Her fondest childhood memories are here. She doesn't know that fruits smell like flowers back home, or that they don't sell much junk food, or that fruit vendors on the street sell sliced mangoes sprinkled with red hot chili powder. Telling her about the red hot chili powder on a sweet ripe mango makes you salivate every time. It does not elicit any reaction from her. You don't bother to tell her about the pineapples back home and how fruit vendors peel the outer skin with machetes and sell them on wooden skewers, or on hot days, sell juices of freshly pulverized pineapples, complete with foam on top. You don't tell her about pineapples back home because she is allergic.

She will do nursing to please you when she grows up, and she will love it most days. It will show her how short life can be and teach her to appreciate the blessings. She will learn about the weakness of the human body and how it lets you down when you need it most. She will be gentle and soften her voice when she talks to you. But there will be days when she comes home with swollen feet and an aching back, and some days she will come home with her ears ringing from patients who hurl ugliness at her because, somehow, her black skin diminishes whatever effort she exerts. If she works fast, she is careless. If she lingers longer with the care, she is lazy.

Your son didn't get too far with his studies even after getting into a top university, and you didn't know he struggled, mostly because you failed to realize that he is a highly sensitive soul. It escaped your notice because there's a language barrier, and there is a cultural barrier too. So you didn't hear his cries for help on those rare occasions when he tried to reach out to you. You were having two different conversations, even though you were talking to each other. He was trying to tell you about the conflicting feelings he was having, but you were lecturing him on the virtues of being strong, of doing right by his parents. You were telling him what a man ought to sacrifice for his family when he was only a boy. When he shared with you his pain of what being black in a place like this does to him, you told him, "You are not that sort of black," and it felt like a slap in his face. You told him that slavery, and the aftermath of hundreds of years, did that to the blacks here. You say 'blacks' the way one would say 'cats' or 'birds,' further dehumanizing his pain, further diminishing his experience. You openly mocked Black Lives Matter and other such movements in front of him, failing to realize that police barrels can't tell one black from another. You failed to realize that you are different than he is. You wear a hijab. You wear a kufi and speak with a thick accent. You never had to endure kids hooting like monkeys when you walked in the school hallways, or you have never been called names like he was. As a kid, no one ever said to you that the sun rises out of Africa every morning, and on the way to the sky, it burned your ass black. Upon hearing something like this, you didn't run home and jump in the shower to try to scrub away the blackness from your skin. And when you failed, you didn't have to face your reflection in the mirror and question why you had to be different.

So when school became too overwhelming, he didn't talk to you about it. It is too bad, because you would have listened. Your eyes have opened now to the unique struggles of children of immigrants. When others shared what they go through with their children, you finally started to see the gray. You no longer operate in the black and white. But still, as a typical African parent, you don't communicate well. You lecture rather than listening, and your anecdotal evidence is always cousins back home who are already married with kids and speak full sentences in Somali when yours can barely get a word out. You constantly mention to your son how his cousin back home stepped up after his father died, and how he now provides for his entire family and his brand-new wife and his brand-new baby. You mention to him how smart and articulate this African cousin is, but you don't know if your son is smart or articulate because the language of his heart is English, and this language of yours is other. How can two hearts fully connect if they don't speak the same?

You only find out about your son when it is too late, when he is expelled from college. Only then do you learn that he could not cope with the stress of your chosen major. You also learn that rather than come to you, he looked for comfort in a bottle and then something stronger and more destructive. While you were tsk-tsking your tongue at wayward children of others from your community, your own was overdosing on alcohol and getting his stomach pumped, and you were not listed as his emergency contact. So you continued your preoccupation with the shortcomings of daughters of others, daughters who show too much skin and laugh too loudly in the company of men.

It surprised you most of all when your son showed up with all his belonging in tow and hunkered down in the basement of your new house, unwilling speak to you for weeks except to give you one-word answers to the questions you ask. You are baffled. You can't understand why he walks around in your house raw and wounded.

139

ANOTHER FORM OF PRAYER
SHAMIMA KHAN

You walk in silence,
In the company of a chipmunk, or a robin
And stop to admire the view in October
The lone maple at the edge of the parking lot
A tree of red stars
Ridiculously beautiful
The world is strange and lovely and painful.
People don't like talking about the pain though,
About being alone,
The problems before us,
Death and what comes after that.

Somehow, with each step you take
You feel closer to God.
How can you not think of the Almighty
When you're in the midst of his bounty,
His creation,
The leaves rustling on the sidewalk,
The smell of green around you,
The steady ground beneath your feet
The air filled with bird song
And as you stop to tie your errant shoelace
You realize
Walking is a form of prayer.

FOUR BOXES
TEHMINA KHAN

for Omar Ali Khan Hutchins

You, Asian Indian from your mother.
You, African-American from your grandfather.
You, Filipino from your great-grandfather.
You, Salvadoran from your great-grandmother.

> You, child of colonial-educated scientists.
> You, child of southern sharecroppers.
> You, child of migrant laborers.
> You, child of domestic workers.

You, with hard work worn into your hands.
You, with trans-continental conquests written in your cells.
You, with migration patterns mapped in blue lines under your skin.

> You, soccer-loving, Spanish-speaking,
> good-at-math, not quite Latino brown boy at mostly brown
> mostly poor middle school in San Francisco.

> You, four boxes checked, white spaces filled,
> on your application to mostly white mostly wealthy
> high school in San Francisco.

A prayer to the One in Arabic.

Silent meditation, observe your thoughts.

> Cook a fusion meal for your family and give thanks.

PART FIVE:
THE HOME
I LEFT

MY MOTHER'S MENU IS STILL MY MENU*
DURAID MUSLEH

I was born in what's known as the West Bank. I am from a village north of Ramallah, called Ajul. It's north of Birzeit, in the middle of the mountains. From the high peaks, you can see the coastline and the Mediterranean from our village.

I grew up under the occupation, getting introduced to the narrative and literature of the revolution against the occupation, the revolutionary poets, and literature and stories and books. The place was buzzing with lectures and discussions and books and movements. So you carry that with you wherever you go. Any suffering the Palestinians went through, we lived it. Wherever you are, you live it regardless. We're always connected. Any war that happens, whether it's in Gaza, or Lebanon, or in Syria these days, your heart goes with the people, whether it's the Arabs or the Palestinians, but especially the Palestinians.

It was very emotional when I went back the first time because I felt this is the only place that I don't need to explain where I came from. Every place you have to explain, I am from Palestine, from the West Bank of Palestine; some people call it Israel. And always people mistaking that with Pakistan. Are you from Pakistan? No, I'm from Palestine. Where is that?...

Growing up, for my dad, their family income was mostly from olive oil production. Our village is famous for its olive oil and is completely covered with olive trees. The olive harvest was an amazing, rich experience for youngsters like me in those days. The mountains are filled at those times with people harvesting. You'd be walking from place to place in the mountains and hear conversations coming from all corners of the orchards. People transport the olives by donkey back. It's primitive, old-fashioned farming. They drop the olives on the field, and the fragrance that comes out of them is a really beautiful smell when they start to disintegrate. So you have this fragrance filling the roads to the village—you call them trails here—and especially to the place where they press it. The whole thing becomes fragrant with olive oil.

My mother used to leave us at our schools in Ramallah and go back to the village to do the harvest season. In the trip she would lose twenty pounds because it's so much hard work for people. It's all manual, and it's the dead winter, very cold, and they have to collect the olives by hand, one at a time, in the mountains. You don't want to do it for a living, unless you are a professional farmer with tools and workers and the rest. It's hard work.

She goes by car and stays in the village for three weeks or four weeks. She loved the olives, and not a season would pass that she would not be part of the effort. She just loved it. It was the income for the family during my father's youthful days. It wasn't big income for us when I was growing up, but my mother felt the sense of responsibility to the trees and the villagers and the heritage, to go and do it by herself every year, even though we just got the supply for the family and some excess to sell. No huge return on this investment of effort, but she just had to do it. It's a religious responsibility or beauty to go and do the olives every year.

I continue to live the simple life that I grew up with. I still eat olive oil and *zatar* every morning for breakfast. This is regular. My mother's menu is still my menu.

* Excerpted and edited from an interview of Duraid Musleh by Najib Joe Hakim (from the "Home Away from Home: Little Palestine by the Bay" Project, 2015.

A HOMELESS OPPRESSED BASTARD
MONIA MAZIGH

Where is home? I have been asking myself this question since I first set foot in Montreal about twenty-eight years ago, and walked in this huge city, a giant compared to my little native town of Tunis, a giant with its straight and long arteries filled with trucks, cars, and snowplows. Nothing in common with Tunisia's tortuous streets and obscure alleys surrounding the old houses like a snake surrounding its prey.

One year after I first arrived in Canada, I went back to visit my parents in Tunisia. It was during the summer and, as usual, I dreaded the heat. Sitting in the sweltering air of my darkened room and longing for some fresh air, I moved my body closer to the wall. But the closer I got to sticking my skin against the wall, the warmer it got and the vainer my attempt. I was bored that summer. Some of my friends were getting married and others were going abroad for studies. And then something strange happened.

One hot night, while I was trying so hard to find some sleep, I felt some movement near my bed. I opened my eyes and tried to figure out what was going on. Was it my brain playing tricks on me or was there a ghost in my room? I saw a shadow moving furtively in the darkness. First, I thought it was my father. Sometimes he would wake up at night and cover me with a blanket when the night got cooler, but it was another hot night, and that couldn't be the case. But the shadow was still there near the entrance of my room. I could see it bending its back and its head, as if it was fixing something in the floor. Once again, I convinced myself it was my father. He must have found one of those summer crickets and was trying to catch it without making a lot of noise. I promised myself that the next morning I would reproach him for his weird idea to catch insects in the middle of the night. But it was not my father. The shadow kept advancing, a crouched silhouette moving toward my bed. In an instant of panic, I realized that it was a stranger, perhaps a thief or a serial killer. I started screaming.

The shadow stopped and quickly ran away, disappearing from my sight back into the darkness of the night. The experience left me stuck with confusion. My parents sleeping in the room next to me hurried to my side, thinking that I had lost my mind, but then they saw me trembling with fear. The stranger left from where he had entered: the door in our living room that opens onto the garden. He had broken in from there; we found the door forced open. We even noticed the footprint marks the stranger had left on our white fence during his escape. The next morning, my father filed a police report. We never found him and never knew why he had entered our home.

I was so frightened, I couldn't sleep in my room anymore. I felt that my privacy was violated, shattered and gone forever. An intruder, a stranger, very likely a man, had been in my room, a few inches away from my bed, from me.

After that night, I started sleeping in the same bed with my mom. My father put a mattress near the living room door where the thief had broken in. My father felt he needed to guard the house. For a few weeks, we lived in terror. Our home dynamics changed as did the rest of my stay in Tunis. When I was about to leave, my mother hugged me and said, "I am so glad you are leaving this place. At least now you won't be scared."

What an irony! I was about to leave my room, my home, my parents, my friends, and my family, and I was 'happy,' or rather relieved. Even my mom was happy to see me leave our home. This beloved place was now equivalent to fear. I was 'happy' because on the other side of the ocean—where people usually looked at me with curious eyes, where I longed for the smell of my mother's cooking—it would be safer or, at least, less scary than in my own room in my native hometown.

Sometimes, your home becomes a place you fear and elsewhere becomes a place you look to for safety. As if the world had gone crazy, as if the earth had abruptly swayed from its normal axis, and as if your mind were racing in the opposite direction.

After that summer, I stopped visiting my hometown. It wasn't because of that incident. I almost forgot about it, but with my demanding graduate studies, life took me in different directions, and I kept postponing my trips to Tunisia. Meanwhile, my parents came to live in Canada, and I considered my visits to Tunis as a luxurious, almost unnecessary, treat.

Until ten years later, when my husband, my two children and I went for a long vacation to Tunis. It was September 2002.

My old house became the house where my Canadian-born children played in the same garden where I played as a child, and sat at night on the same veranda where I used to lay down over a *kilim*, gazing at the stars, trying to catch the shooting ones. Then, when my husband decided to go back home to Ottawa for his job, my childhood home brought me some comfort, like a soft lullaby swaying me between sad and nice memories.

But not for long. In a few days, my life scrambled before my very eyes when I learned that my husband had been arrested by the American authorities and thrown into prison. He became a casualty of the so-called war on terror. My world collapsed. My old home couldn't help me stay calm, couldn't give me any answers to the Kafkaesque journey that was unfolding in front of me.

I was confused, scared, enraged, and terrorized. I felt like a hostage of that same house, its walls, its small windows and fuzzy garden. I was no longer living in the time zone of Tunis, but rather was constantly waiting for the North American continent to wake up. My only quest was to speak to Canadian officials and try to learn more about the whereabouts of my husband.* None of my relatives and friends knew what had happened. I kept it as a secret, as if I was ashamed of what had happened to him. I was alone with my children. My home couldn't protect me anymore. My memories were kidnapped by this new harsh reality. I needed a home, so I flew back to Ottawa.

Snowstorms, winds, blizzards, Ottawa rivers, parkways, Parliament Hill. They became my new friends. My old friends, the ones I once knew, were scared by the news. They hid from me. They fell silent.

My house became smaller and smaller. Few people wanted to come to my home. I was the wife of the terrorist. My children were the children of the terrorist. My home was the home of the terrorist. My mother came to live with us. She cooked for us, helped with the children, and most of all, loved us. She became our home, the home whose calming bosom we put our heads on to find peace and serenity.

Today, when I go back to Tunis, walking within those same tortuous streets and dirty alleys, I look so intently, my sight penetrating the faces of people, trying to identify a friend, an old neighbor, or even a former teacher. Nothing. All of the faces are strangers. They are busy with their lives; they don't even look back at me. For them, I look like any other Tunisian woman. Even the headscarf that I decided to put on my head when I turned twenty, in a decision of wholeheartedly accepting my Islamic faith and spirituality, no longer distinguishes me from all the other women. In Tunis of 1990, a hijab on the head of a middle-class young woman was rare and unusual. I used to be one of the handful of students at Institute of Hautes Études Commerciales who wore a hijab. In the early '90s, in the crowded streets of Tunis, in the crammed yellow buses, few women dared to wear the hijab; it was portrayed by the President Zine Al Abidine ben Ali and his government as a sign of extremism or political affiliation with the Islamist movement.

This narrative didn't start in the '90s. It started a long time ago when Habib Bourguiba, the father of the nation, the one who brought its independence in 1956, linked progress to staunch secularism. Any sign of religiosity was considered a sign of backwardness. Praying was associated with irrationality. Fasting was synonymous with laziness. Modesty for women was equated with oppression. In order to be progressive and modern, we were told to align ourselves with France, the mother of civilizations, and the country that colonized us or maybe 'protected' us. We had to love France, love its language, read it, speak it, and embrace everything that comes with it. A product of my generation, I was not any different. I loved French culture with passion and determination.

But I always kept a secret love, a love of mosques. I loved listening to the silence of their empty spaces punctuated by the ticking sounds of the bead rosaries. I loved listening to the beautiful recitations of the Arabic words of the Qur'an. I loved contemplating the humongous chandelier of the Zitouna mosque in the heart of the Medina of Tunis, wondering about the skillful hands that crafted it and brought it up there to illuminate the nights of our prayers. I loved hearing the little voices in me that kept linking me to the earth of this land that saw successive civilizations destroyed and others built: Phoenicia, Carthage, Rome, Kairouan, Andalusia, Istanbul and many others. I heard their moaning in my heart.

In the Tunis of the 2010s, I was not an object of curiosity or suspicion anymore. The headscarf was part of the new urban landscape. Years of oppression, years of attempts to remove any signs of religiosity had failed miserably. To the contrary, it brought about an overreaction. People were thirsty to know their history, their roots, their language, and to adopt the religion of their mothers and grandmothers. They couldn't find it at home; they couldn't find it in school; they couldn't find it at work, so, for many, they found it on satellite TV.

These devices were everywhere, from the upscale neighborhoods of Carthage to the slum cities of Kabbaria. Every house, every apartment, and every shack had a satellite dish to capture all the channels that exploded in the Arab world and elsewhere during the '90s. With them appeared all the preachers who spoke directly to women in their living rooms and bedrooms. They spoke to them, unlike their teachers who didn't pay attention to them or their mothers who didn't have time for them. They answered their questions, quenching their thirst for 'knowledge.' Satellite TV channels taught people everything. From how to cook a fancy Lebanese dish to how to pray. It was a cacophony of voices. Good ones and bad ones, reasonable ones and extremist ones. But amidst these voices, the identity issue became central. And many women choose to wear a headscarf as a way to mend fences with their lost identity. Dictators have plans for tiny details of people's lives, but they have no plans for satellite dishes and a strong quest for belonging.

With these changes, waves of women started dressing modestly in the streets, on public transportation and even on beaches. The burkinis that used to be sold under the counter, fearing that the store owner would be accused of sympathy with the Islamist party, were now sold in Carrefour stores, the heart of neoliberal economic implementation in Tunisia.

Nevertheless, despite these new waves of women in hijab, I realized that I was a stranger. I had nothing in common with these women who looked like me, dressed like me, and spoke the dialect I grew up speaking. I don't have many friends left, and even the dialect I spoke is now considered outdated and old fashioned compared to the panoply of new words that have emerged via talk show radio and rap music.

During my years of activism against the national security legislation, the anti-terrorism laws, and the security certificates that mainly targeted Arab and Muslim communities after 9/11, I had, on several occasions, spoken at churches across Canada, places where these issues can be safely denounced without necessarily being considered as an apology for terrorism. Doing so in mosques would raise suspicion or would literally put you in trouble. Mosques were demonized, spied on, and even vandalized. I found in churches a receptive audience and a calming effect that reminded me of my youthful love of mosques. So, ironically, I came to love the churches too. They represent a place of worship, but also a place of resistance. Resistance to the oppression of invading laws and of the times themselves that no longer give us any space for respite, breath, contemplation and reflection.

Many times, people ask me: In which language do you think? And each time, I have the same surprised reaction. I promise myself to pay more attention to the language I am thinking in, and yet each time I forget, or maybe my mind makes me unconsciously forget.

Words are confusing, exactly like identities. When I go out in public, do I really think of who I am ? A Canadian? A Muslim? A woman with a hijab? A mother? A wife of a torture survivor? An immigrant? How to live with all these identities at the same time? Emphasizing one, dropping another, keeping one at a low profile, boasting about another, or amalgamating and juggling all of them together and trying to be at peace?

When I tell people that I am African, they frown at me with dismay, thinking it's a bad joke. So why am I not black? they would ask. And I'd quickly add that I am North African. That slight adjustment makes my assertion more credible, but nevertheless still confusing. In fact, being a North African is problematic today, especially in France. But that is another story.

My mother tongue is Arabic, but my family name is Berber, or Amazigh. The Amazigh were the indigenous tribes that roamed the vast lands of North Africa. They called themselves the 'free men.' So literally, I am a free woman. But still, with my hijab, I am constantly described as an oppressed woman. Then when I meet North Africans with Berber origins, their first question to me is: do you speak Amazigh? When I sheepishly respond no, I am immediately considered a false indigenous. A traitor. A cultural failure. An assimilated product. Someone with an empty shell, deprived from her deep Berber syllables. Something of the sort of the Islamness or blackness of Barack Obama…

But even for Arab-speaking people, I can barely pass the test. I am Tunisian, and the Arabic dialect I speak is filled with some French words. So, for the purist Arab Mideasterners like my in-laws, I speak some sort of French, and for the purist French people, I speak some sort of Arabic. As you can see, I can never win. I am a can of contradictions. I am a bastard. I don't have a language. I am an oppressed woman. I don't choose what to wear. I am homeless; I don't have a home.

Arriving in Québec as an immigrant, it didn't make my life easier that I didn't have the Québecois accent; that was considered a problem for my integration. Not only was my accent problematic, but also my appearance as a hijabi is considered a sign of female oppression and alienation. Apparently, I have some paranormal powers: wherever I go, my hijab shatters years of women's struggle. No matter how hard I worked to prove the opposite and join the 'us,' I was always considered the 'other.'

So finally, I moved to Ontario and discovered the genius of multiculturalism as introduced by Pierre Trudeau, the father of our 'cool' Prime Minister Justin Trudeau. I thought that my multiple identity crises would be buried forever. Unfortunately for me and for the world, the 9/11 attacks happened, and since then, I have been judged and looked upon through the deforming lens of terrorism.

Today, I write to better understand the world and myself. I write in English, a language I started learning in high school while listening to Madonna. You can understand that even Shakespeare would distance himself from me. I write in French, not the one my in-laws think I am speaking, but the real French. Well, hopefully! I keep reading a lot in Arabic, and guess what. I still don't know in which language I think.

Tunis, my home town, has changed, and I have changed too. Even my old home has changed. It disappeared, demolished by bulldozers and turned into rubble. It got replaced by a luxurious house with a tall gate, two floors, and a basement. "There is even a swimming pool," added the owner of the *dépanneur* close to our old home, who used to report everything about the neighbours to the police agents parked in the station a few meters down our street. This time, he reported this news to my mother, who had come to visit one of her old neighbours. She thought a swimming pool was a bit too much. I agreed. And even the *centre d'achat* that we, my teenager friends and I, thought was the coolest place on earth, even more glamourous than the Galleries Lafayette in Paris, was now ugly for my eyes. I found it full of garbage containers, scattered empty plastic bottles, and potholes in the parking lot. I don't know if it is my Canadian adult eyes that have gotten used, over the years, to nicer places and cleaner environments; eyes that are becoming pickier and finding issues with what used to be a sign of coolness and progress in my teenage years. After all, infrastructure isn't progress; it decays if it isn't maintained.

The same thing happens to homes. They also decay if they aren't maintained.

* Maher Arar, is a Canadian citizen of Syrian descent. In 2002, he was arrested on his way to Montreal by the American authorities at the JFK airport. They later forcibly rendered him to Syria via Jordan. He was imprisoned for over a year where he was tortured and kept in solitary confinement. Maher Arar was never charged with any crime by any country. His wife, Monia Mazigh, led a public campaign in Canada asking for his release. He was released in 2003 and was repatriated to Canada. In 2004, the Canadian government announced a public inquiry into the case of Maher Arar. In 2006, Maher Arar was cleared by the public inquiry of any terrorism association. The Canadian government apologized to him and his family and compensated him for his ordeal.

THE HOME I LEFT
TAYYABA SYED

Pakistan, you're a foreign land to me.
I may have called you home once but then life took me another way.
I don't know you or remember much of you.
Yet you still run through my veins to this day.

The sustenance that formed my flesh and bones grew from your earth.
The first air that entered my lungs came from your trees.
The first soil that met my feet bore from your ground.
The water that quenched my first thirst flowed directly from your springs.

You are of me, and I am of you.
I may have left you, but you never left me.
I wait for the day I return home and lay my eyes upon you again,
And what seems so foreign now becomes fully part of me again.

BINT AL QUDS,* DAUGHTER OF JERUSALEM
SAMAR NAJIA

You had no say in choosing it, but how perfectly it fit. The first thing you ever owned, immortalized on a birth certificate. So many have tried and failed to erase it, disguise it, anglophile it. In sickness and in health, it sticks with you 'til the bitter end.

"It is the crown I wear," she says. "Do you know who I am?"

I do. I've learned so much about you by the mere knowledge of your name. It is the alphabet of your being, a history of your kin. It shields you in obscurity in your adopted land, and propels you to falsified fame amid new found friends. It is the key to a diary, to a memory you would lend. It is abandoned destinies, and fractured families you kept hidden from my pen.

"I am *Bint Al Quds*," she tells me as though for the first time, "Daughter of Jerusalem. I am from the Holy Land."

How can I forget the story you repeat? Suleiman the Magnificent walked victoriously through your streets, and upon your family he bestowed a lifelong guardianship of the land. Faithful sentries you stood at King David's Tomb. Five centuries doubled to eternity while your name echoed in its corridors.

"My name is my story, and my forefathers' before," she says. "The only coin left in my pocket when we left Holy Land."

There you go again, one hundred times a day, as though I would forget. "Daughter of Jerusalem, *Bint Al Quds*," you breathe it into the phone. Loud and clear, I hear it. That subtle pride in your voice. I listen to your sadness and feel the rising boast.

The heritage of your name was a birthright now utterly lost.

"And so, it is, why do you protest? My name is an ever companion amid foreign lands and fickle hands."

But what a heavy burden to carry, the grand personas of your forefathers who gave the city life. Leave their shadows behind in the old city quarters. Show me the humanity beneath. That person I love so well. No need to talk of the dead because it will impress. Why ride the coattails of history, when you are so grand yourself?

"It's been so hard, so hard," she says. "Jerusalem is in my blood, not just my name."

But it is only a small part of who you are. It means nothing to most. Do you not see that you are my queen, whatever your name may be? Your name is just one of many mothers and teachers to me. It makes for neither cloak nor guise when you weep for the home you lost. Stand high, stand alone, free of the entanglements of your name *Ya Bint Al Quds*, daughter of the Holy Land.

"Never. Never," she says. "I am the daughter of the motherland. I am its daughter 'til the bitter end."

OVERSEAS
HALAH BUTT

Karachi, Pakistan's most populated port city, overflows with crowded streets, people, noise and litter. Locals dressed in *shalwar kameez*, traditional Pakistani dresses, weave through car-packed streets in blues, greys and pinks, between buildings browned with dust. High-pitched car horns blare over the shouts of street vendors selling plastic toys and jasmine bracelets, straggle-toothed beggars and dancing men dressed as women. To the general public, Pakistan means Taliban, terrorists, Osama bin Laden. But it's where my mother was born and brought up, where her parents live, where we have family reunions every six years. My parents met and got married in Karachi. Dad was visiting family after mountain climbing in the north, and Mom was about to enroll in art school. They met at a friend's house and got married three months later. I've heard the story a thousand times.

Karachi is the place I have to use as my answer after people ask, "No, but what's your background?" because "born in Toronto" doesn't make sense to them. I've only visited Karachi three times, each time with a span of six years in between. From those three times, the most distinct memories include hours of watching the Disney Channel, FIFA, and Master Chef with my cousins, looking for and taking care of stray cats, and shooting at lizards with plastic BB guns. These moments are underlined by the constant putrid smell of pollution, witnessing a shocking number of beggars and homeless, and falling sick despite staying clear of street food and tap water.

It took Mom a month and a big fight to convince Dad to let our 2014 summer trip to Karachi last two months and not just one. Dad argued that his work would only give him a one- or two-week vacation. He couldn't stand being alone for the rest of the time. Mom replied that she hadn't been back home for six years, that it was her eldest niece's wedding, and that it was the first family wedding since theirs, twenty years ago.

Lying in my Ammi's, grandmother's, guest room, sick with a cold and flu three weeks into our visit, I don't blame Dad's resentment. The a/c unit over the bed hums, a cold draft of moist air cooling the room. Water droplets drip from a leak inside. I stare at the four white ceiling fans whirling around until my head begins to ache. I turn to my side with a groan and squint from the bright sliver of the outside world visible behind thick bronze curtains layered in front of the window. All the curtains here are thick and heavy, because apparently the heat goes through glass. If I stood behind the large drapes, it would be five degrees hotter than the rest of the room.

My eyes adjust to the light. Green leaves of a palm tree touch the dusty glass window. A faded blue sky outlines the white flat rooftops of the neighboring houses. It's recess, and the muffled cries of preschool children on the playground travel upstairs. Ammi has been running a preschool in her house for thirty-five years. A classroom on each side of the house and one inside make up *Tibna's Nursery*. I hold a pillow over my head. The a/c, the fans, and the kids shouting make my head throb. The noise pulses in my blocked ears.

I miss the quiet. At home in the Milton suburbs, the only sounds come from the faint whisper of traffic, the low hum of the house's furnace. Here, with around twenty people staying in one house, everyone shouts over each other to get their voice heard. The TV is constantly on, either on a 12-hour cricket match or the current news of Pakistani politics. The cricket-player-turned-politician Imran Khan is leading marches against the corrupt system or something. The worst is the television commercials. Pakistani actors with light skin and flowing hair uttering phrases in accented English advertising, "*Limu Pani*, lemon water, all the freshness!"

"Golden Pearl Beauty Queen, lighten your skin!"

"Black Bourbon! Black Bourbon!"

Someone knocks on the door and I peer down the long rectangular room. Bibi walks in carrying a basket of clothes, a purple shawl loosely wrapped around her head and shoulders. Bibi is Ammi's *nokri* which translates as maid. Mom says she's like her sister more than anything. I close my eyes, pretending to be asleep. While the cousins sit around watching Master Chef, Bibi folds all the laundry. She cleans the bathrooms, sweeps the floor. The floors need to be cleaned every few hours because of all the dust, with a brush made of long twigs. You have to crouch down on your knees to use it.

Bibi places the basket of laundry on the ottoman that sits on the other side of the room. Hangers clack together as she hangs the clothes in the large cupboards near the door. When it's empty she picks up the basket and leaves, closing the door quietly behind her. I prop myself up on my elbows and sigh. I never thought I'd voluntarily want to do housework.

The muffled chatter of the kids dies down as they return to class. It must be two o'clock. I roll off the bed, grab a glass from the bedside table, and shuffle to the water cooler at the end of the room. The glass feels cool in my hand as it fills. I walk back to the bed and push open the purple bathroom door on my left. Ammi painted the whole left wall a Barbie purple. The heavy door closes behind me and I'm overwhelmed by the heat. Only the bedrooms and the living room are individually air conditioned. The rest, the hall, the class rooms and the kitchen, use ceiling fans. The bathrooms have small windows.

I walk over to the sink. The narrow, blue-tiled space reflects in the mirror above it. A shower head sticks out of the wall at the very end. There's no tub and no dividing line that separates the shower from the rest of the floor. Instead, water splashes everywhere and then escapes through a small drain in the middle of the bathroom. I turn on the sink faucet and wash my face, careful not to swallow, then use the water in the glass to rinse my mouth. There's recently been a warning of bacteria in the tap water.

The glass clinks loudly on the porcelain sink as I set it down. My head spins from the overbearing, suffocating heat. The bathroom was built just before we arrived, and the ceiling is still just wooden beams and metal poles, with sunlight and humidity seeping from the sunroof. My hands clench the edges of the sink as black dots flicker in the corners of my sight. My legs go numb and I retch from the empty feeling in my stomach. I stumble towards the door, shove it open, and quickly fall onto the bed. Head throbbing, I close my eyes. Orange and yellow spots dance inside my eyelids, and the sudden cold of the a/c makes me shiver.

I wish I took Dad's side in the argument.

GARDENIA COMFORT
REEM HAMMAD

Siham had decided to hold still, to stay home. After several
failed attempts to reach her by phone a day earlier, I finally get through,
and she is delighted to hear my voice. She sounds burdened and
frustrated but is warmed by the words she hears: " Happy Birthday,
Soussou!" I chant to her. A moment of silence and then an outpouring
of joy mixed with sadness comes out to me across the many miles that
now separate us.

She had forgotten her birthday, forgotten which day it was,
which year or which war she is living through. She is not panicked but
sounds overcome with shock. "Not again!" she says in frustration, and
then briefs me on the state of chaos that has struck Beirut, people
rushing to stock up on food, medicine and water, electric outages here
and there, families rushing to the aid of their loved ones, a state of
emergency quite familiar to the Lebanese people hardened from years
of war.

She asks about my journey back home and says how glad she
is that I made it out of Beirut before the disaster hit. I ask her to leave
the city, to get out whenever the American Embassy begins to evacuate
its citizens, but she stays silent. She is there to stay. She will never leave
Beirut, will never leave her ailing old mother, her home, her sense of
pride and safety. She will stay. She will wake up each morning, will
stand on her balcony overlooking the city and watch the now silent
streets of Beirut that, a few days earlier, were bustling with the energy
of summer tourists, lively merchants, busy restaurants and an endless
web of traffic. Today the sky is thickly grey, the air heavy, humid, with
sticky smoke residue. Siham awakens again out of her morning gaze
with the rushing sound of cars whizzing through the empty streets, and
is reminded of more pressing duties. She will dress quickly and rush out
her door. She will go to see Ni'mat, her mother, who lives a few miles
away from her.

Ni'mat lives in an old Lebanese-style house built out of stone, with elegant arched windows and entryways, a beautiful flower-filled courtyard with a water fountain at its heart. She lives alone with her helper, a young Sri Lankan woman who cares for her basic needs day and night. Ni'mat is still asleep when Siham arrives. She has slept longer than usual today. She had a hard time falling asleep the night before for she had missed the rocking melodies and loud sounds coming from the tight quarters of her neighborhood. This past night was an unusually silent night. Although Ni'mat is struck with Alzheimer's disease and her memory is mostly gone, she had felt something different and could not close her eyes until the familiar noise started again this morning. Siham is concerned, but for once she is in full realization of something she never thought of before. She realizes the blessing of her mother's disease on a grim day like this one. Her mother is in a different world, no sense of time, no sense of change. She has no clue what disaster has befallen her beloved Lebanon just two days earlier.

She is sound asleep in her bed now, tucked in her fresh white linen sheets. On her side table rests a small glass of water with three fresh cuttings of gardenia flowers. The scent fills the air of her high-ceiling, darkened room. Siham stands by the doorway lovingly admiring the stillness in her mother's room, the tranquility she felt in this same house as she herself was growing up. She is safe and this is home, and that is what will keep her here in Beirut.

ALHUWIYYA (THE IDENTITY)
GHADEER ELGHAFRI

I am from a *mubaraka* (holy) tree,
zaytouna (olive tree) not in the east, not in the west,
zayt, zaatar, duga (olive oil, thyme and duqqa),
teen (figs) clinging on to old walls,
and farms of lemons and oranges.
Baladi (my homeland's) weather is pleasant
and *baharha* (its sea) is clear.

I am from the Arabian Gulf *nakhla* (palm),
stable roots,
branches in the sky,
sahra wa jemal (desert and camels),
humidity and hot sun,
kahwa wa tammer (coffee and dates),
oil and towers.

I am from *alqayiqap* (the maple) tree
and maple syrup.
My leaves are changing colors —
red, yellow, orange
as *huwiyyati* (my identity) changes.
My leaves fall in autumn
as my age falls
away from *alwatan* (the homeland).

PART SIX: UNDER THE BLUE TENT

I AM MARYAM
MARYAM SABRI*

I am the cotton candy blue
Mediterranean sea,
its silky stars in the night sky.
I am flying fire and waterfall magic
misting down to Lac De Gafsa Lake.
I am a volcano sunset on Raf Raf erupting with light,
its diamond waves shining bright.
I am Atlas Mountain oasis water and midnight light.

I come from a land of beach and extraordinary history
called TUNISIA.
Tunisia my Paris;
Tunisia my home.
I am of Roman and French colonizers.
I am the Berber before the Arabians came.
I am of people knowing and caring for each other.
I am spicy yummy *couscous* with *brik*,
magical street food
and sweet teensy *Kolow* pieces with tiny white chocolate nuts.
I am of aqua and teal tropical water, palm trees,
and powdered sugar sand;
fine clean white *Sidi Bou Said* buildings capped with white arches
and the white domed roofs of Greece;
ocean blue doors and lapis colored windows,
where we can play soccer in safe narrow streets,
go to market by ourselves for toast in the morning,
ice cream in the afternoon.
I am the birth of the Star Wars Tatooine desert terrain scapes
with mud sand buildings.

I am the hot Sahara
and a citizen of America.
I am discovery;
the next Ibn Battuta,
your upcoming travel agent,
your future president.

I am Maryam Sabri.

Maryam Sabri is 9 years old.

WHITE ISMAILI
AQUIL VIRANI

I was getting dressed in my bedroom, with a collared white shirt and grey dress pants, when my mom yelled to me from the other room. "Remember Aquil..." she said in her Parisian accent. "It's *Khushyali* tonight!" While I had been preparing for another routine visit to Saturday mosque, this was a welcomed jolt of much-needed excitement. We would instead be heading downtown to Vancouver's Pacific Coliseum for a yearly celebration with thousands of other Shia Ismaili Muslims. As a seven-year-old boy, I wasn't eager to go for the religious ceremonies or even the sugary cake; I was a young kid who just wanted to show off my energetic dancing skills to any adults who would watch. Tonight, I was going to shine.

With a name like Aquil, I had stood out since my peppy pre-school teacher, Anita, first said my name during attendance. I had explained to her that I had an Indian father and a French mother who had given me an Arabic name because we were Muslim. "Are you sure you mean Indian?" she asked me. "Because, Aquil, you look very white." As a child, it was never very clear to me what was so confusing. I simply knew I was telling the truth and happy to be both Indian and French.

Hearing the distant bass of the thumping speakers from the parking lot, I rushed ahead of my parents towards the coliseum entrance where two *khoja* volunteers were ushering the *jamaat* into the arena. They stopped me at the door. "Excuse me, kid, this is an Ismaili function. It is not for the general public."

I didn't know immediately what was happening. At first, I felt the way a young child does when they "get in trouble"—both guilty and overwhelmed. And then it was clear. I was a white boy who didn't look like everyone else. I didn't resemble my Indian or Afghani friends. These volunteers assumed that I didn't belong.

As my French mother approached from behind me in a traditional sari, the volunteers must have realized their mistake and quickly disappeared. I began to notice the peculiar attention that my white-skinned mother attracted from other Ismailis in the corridor. She pointed me in the direction of the live music where I could dance away the night and charm the masses with my enthusiastic dancing.

Later, as the live musicians announced their last song of the night, the lead singer on stage asked if there were a few volunteers who wanted to join them on the platform to dance in front of the entire arena. Recognizing my face from hours before, the leader of the band asked me directly if I would like to come up. Even though I had been dreaming of such an opportunity, in that young moment, I understood something important about visibility and the "model minority" that has guided me ever since. "I don't want to go up," I said. I won't be seen for me.

They'll just see a white Ismaili.

Author's note: This story comes from a personal lived experience. That being said, as someone who is often seen as white, I acknowledge the white privilege (or light skin privilege) that I benefit from and I declare proudly and confidently that "reverse racism isn't a thing." It's not the same to feel excluded or be treated differently when you're (seen as) part of a dominant group. I think that nuance is important to include here. Thanks for reading.

UNDER THE BLUE TENT
AMBATA KAZI-NANCE

Fouad opened the chamber of the gun and set it on the dresser, staring at the empty slots. His hand moved to the three scars that ran across his left forearm just below the inside of his elbow. He picked up the gun and loaded it with six bullets. He only needed one to do the job, but this way was easier. No risk of mistakes. He was going to end his life. But first, he had to take his son to the circus.

He'd found the advertisement a few days ago. His mailbox had been stuffed with coupon catalogues. He was about to toss the bundle into the garbage when a small, waxy slip of paper fell at his feet. *Blue Tent Circus*, the flyer read. *Fun, Adventure, and Excitement Awaits Under the Blue Tent.*

Fouad hadn't planned to see his son, Samir, before he killed himself. He and his ex-wife, Maritza, had an informal agreement that allowed him two weekends a month with his son. He skipped out on most of his weekends though, claiming he had a plumbing gig, even long after his license had been revoked, when really he was nursing a hangover or gearing up for a bender.

He wanted to see Samir, but he didn't want Samir to see him. He knew he couldn't be around his son when he was drunk, but sober wasn't good either. Sober, he couldn't control his thoughts, which spun like a demonic dervish. Sadness brought anger, his anger frightened him, fear made him nervous. It was a spiral, ever tightening. Only alcohol could loosen it, just a little. He knew it was best for Samir that he wasn't around.

But looking at the circus ticket, Fouad had a vision. He saw himself and Samir at the circus. Samir's eyes lighting up watching the elephants and tigers perform tricks, Samir jumping up and down and clapping when Fouad won him prizes at the game booths, Samir looking up at him with a beaming smile at the end of the day, hugging him and thanking him again and again. The vision shifted to an adult Samir finding his tattered circus ticket in an old keepsake box and showing it to his children, telling his kids about the grandfather they'd never met, a troubled man but a man who had tried, who had given Samir the best day of his life.

Fouad surged with renewed energy. It would take all the mental strength he could gather, but he could stay sober for a few hours and be a good dad for once. He could leave his son with a good memory of him, then go home and put a bullet in his head and finally shatter the spiral.

He called Maritza and asked if he could take Samir. He wasn't sure if it was his weekend or not, but she said yes. Rather than pleasing him, her quick acceptance made him angry. Just once he wished she'd curse him out like he deserved, call him a no-good drunk, a complete fuck-up of a husband and father, but no, she was patient with him, blandly and indifferently patient with him, just as she always was.

On a Saturday afternoon, Fouad pulled up in front of the house that used to be his. His mouth filled with saliva. Nausea simmered in his gut. He ran his fingers over the scars on his arm, pressing gently, forcing himself to breathe deeply. The house had been a faded, peeling white when he and Maritza bought it. He'd never gotten around to painting it, like Maritza had asked repeatedly, but now it was a creamy peach sorbet with a Caribbean blue trim. A cobblestone walkway wended a path to the front door. Daisies and violets hung from baskets above the porch. It looked nothing like the house Fouad remembered; it had become a home.

The side of the driveway that had been Fouad's sat empty. Ben, the new husband, was out, probably getting groceries or buying tools for the next home improvement project. Ben had a jolly beard the color of rust, and he was always fixing things.

Maritza answered at his knock. Her face was serene and unsmiling, her dark hair pulled back in a neat ponytail. She wore a long black skirt and a loose white tunic. Fouad remembered a time when she'd worn miniskirts and lacy low-cut tops, her hair spilling down in waves to her waist like a mermaid.

They had been wild together, slamming shots of tequila at bars and sneaking into dirty alleyways when they could no longer control themselves. Fouad thought they'd been escaping life together, reveling in being unmoored, but it turned out Maritza wasn't running away, she was waiting to be found. Pregnant with Samir, she became curious about the book in a strange script Fouad kept in a dresser drawer, never opened, asked him to read something from it, and fell in love with the words. She'd gulped the holy text like a dying fish returned to water and never even glanced back at the land she'd left behind.

They'd stayed together for a while after Maritza converted. She'd been patient, even teasing, trying to persuade him to pray with her, to go to the *masjid* with her. Then she began to sigh whenever Fouad reached for a bottle, and though he took his bottles and skulked out to the backyard, her sighs carried out into the dark, until the night she stood at the back door, balancing Samir on her hip, and told Fouad she couldn't live like this anymore. They divorced and she met and married Ben, a new convert like herself, just before Samir's second birthday, when he was still young enough to adapt seamlessly to the new life Maritza shaped for them. Studying Maritza's bare, smooth face, Fouad realized he had never really known her.

"Samir," she called over her shoulder. "Your dad is here." She turned back to Fouad. "How are you?" she asked.

"Hanging in there. You?"

"*Alhamdulillah.*"

"Right."

Without trying to, she crushed him, reminding him of where he came from. Here in America, with his brown skin and hair that rolled into tight curls if he didn't cut it every other week, people thought he was black. And it was easier to let people think that, since they couldn't say or spell Mauritania, let alone find it on a map. He could almost forget about all that made him foreign, until Maritza brought him back.

Samir's footsteps galloping down the stairs triggered the spiral inside Fouad. He hadn't seen his son in months. His hands trembled. Sweat popped out of his pores. He felt cold and hot at the same time. He chided himself to stay in control. Samir appeared at Maritza's side, clutching a book to his chest. He was eight years old, all gangly arms and legs, his face a mirror image of his father's. He smiled shyly at Fouad. The spiral loosened.

"Hey, kiddo," Fouad said.

Samir stepped to him, his free hand pulling at the hem of his T-shirt. Fouad lifted his hand to shake his son's at the same time the boy leaned in. They settled into a stiff, one-armed hug.

"You ready to go to the circus?" Fouad asked.

Samir scuffed his shoes on the welcome mat. He pressed at the spine of his book. "I don't know if I like the circus."

Fouad's stomach clenched. Samir was supposed to be excited. Already the vision was losing luster, the edges darkening and curling. He felt Maritza's eyes on him, measuring him. "Well, here's your chance to find out," he tried.

Samir's eyes widened. "Like a science experiment?" he asked.

"Yep. Exactly."

"Okay."

Samir turned back to his mother and dug his head into the center of her chest. She pulled his face into her hands and kissed his cheeks and forehead then hugged him, whispering prayers over his head.

Fouad's mother had been the same way with him and his siblings, never letting them leave the house, not even to play outside, without praying for them. She was a sad, anxious mother, out of place in America and nostalgic for home, prone to weeping and long spells at the window. She'd held tightly to her cultural and religious identity. The prideful tilt of her chin as she wrapped her hijab in front of the mirror, the ease in her gait as she walked the streets of their small Connecticut town in her traditional clothes, oblivious to the stares she received. Prayer and fasting held her steady. She had a place she could call home, on Earth and in the spiritual realm. Fouad had neither.

Maritza finally pulled away from Samir.

"Have a good time, sweetheart," she said.

She looked at Fouad. "Have him home by six, please."

Fouad nodded. Maritza shut the door. Walking to his truck, Fouad knew she was watching them. He opened the door for Samir and waited until his seat belt was fastened.

Thankfully the engine cranked up without a hiccup. He eased the truck onto the street and drove slowly out of the neighborhood.

"Dad."

"Yeah?"

"Who's Fred J?"

"What?"

"The sign on your truck. Who's Fred J?

"Oh, well, that's me."

Samir had never seen him in his work truck. Up till recently, he'd picked him up in the Mustang. He scratched the stubble on his cheek.

"It's easier to get a plumbing job when your name is Fred J. and not Fouad Jabbar." He laughed and looked over at the boy, but his face was solemn.

"So," Samir asked slowly, "you lie about it?"

Fouad sputtered. "It's not a lie. I just changed it a little, just for work. Like a—like a nickname. You don't get called Sammy or Sam at school?"

Samir shook his head. "No. Some kids try to, even some teachers, but I don't let them. I tell them that is not my name." He shrugged. "I like my name."

"Yeah? That's good," Fouad said.

He slumped in his seat. His own kid had more confidence at eight years old than he'd ever had in his whole life. Kids at school used to call him Food. "What's up, Food?" they'd say, passing him in the hallways, stretching out the vowels so that it sounded like a cow mooing. In the cafeteria, "Hey Food, want some food?" Or Gum Wad. That one had started in high school when a teacher, trying to pronounce his name correctly, had said, "Oh, Foo-wad, like a wad of gum." The class had erupted in laughter; Fouad's ears had burned. They were stupid jokes, stupid nicknames he should have been able to shrug off, but they'd brought on an anger so intense that he'd taken a kitchen knife and sliced into his arm just to release it.

Anger and shame twisted Fouad's gut like a wet towel. The beginning of a headache thumped at the top of his head. There was a flask of whiskey in the glove compartment, but no, he couldn't do that. He searched the distance in front of him, frantic. Golden arches loomed.

"You hungry?" he asked. "Want some McDonald's?"

"Mommy says we can't eat there. She says the meat's not *halal*."

Fouad stifled a sigh. "Alright, how about some fries at least? A coke? A milkshake?"

Samir grinned. "Milkshake," he whispered.

"Good deal." Fouad extended his fist and Samir bumped it with his own.

Fouad and Samir sat in a corner booth. Samir gripped his chocolate milkshake with both hands, sipping it steadily. Fouad picked at his fries, his burger with only one small bite taken. His appetite, always erratic, had slowed even more recently.

Samir slurped up the last of his milkshake with a loud gurgle. A group of old men a few tables away chuckled, grinning at Samir and then Fouad, their smiles tender and knowing. Fouad saw himself through the men's eyes, a father taking his son out to lunch, a father and son sharing a simple, special moment. He picked up his burger and took a big bite. He chewed slowly, savoring the crunchy tang of the pickle against the sweetness of the ketchup. He smiled to himself and took a few more bites, relishing this unexpected hunger.

Samir put his empty cup down and laid his hands in his lap. Fouad pushed his box of fries towards Samir. He slid one out and frowned at it.

"Daddy, how come you never take me to your house?"

The food in Fouad's mouth turned rotten. He wanted to spit it out. Fouad didn't have a house or even an apartment, just a room he rented from some stone-faced Honduran guys who eyed him with suspicion whenever he was around and never spoke to him. He had a tiny bedroom with one sad window just below the ceiling that offered only feeble light. He kept it clean, but with the cracks in the walls and the dingy brown carpet, there was nothing he could do to stop it from looking like a prison cell.

"Ah, my place is a sh—, it's not a good place for a kid. Too small."

"Ben says our house is too small, too. He says we should get another house before the baby comes."

Fouad gripped his seat and dug his nails into the vinyl cushion, wishing it were his own flesh. His fingers found the scars and jabbed at them, the scar tissue too thick to break through without something sharp. He caught Samir looking at the scars and covered them with his hand.

He cleared his throat. "So your mom's having a baby, huh?"

"Yeah, I can't wait." Samir smiled dreamily. "I hope I get a little brother." He paused in his chewing. "Do you have any brothers and sisters?"

Fouad looked into the well of his son's eyes. He had a brother and a sister. A mother and a father. The last he'd talked to any of them, they were all still in Connecticut, but that was years ago, almost two decades really. That was the truth, but so was the fact that leaving them and clearing his tracks was probably the one good thing he'd ever done for them.

"No," he answered. "Just me."

He watched Samir eat the fries, one after the other, his jaw bobbing up and down. He would leave a note with their names and addresses.

Fouad grabbed a napkin and wiped at the grease and ketchup smeared on Samir's cheek. "Alright, buddy, ready to see some lions, and tigers, and bears?"

Samir's eyes grew wide. "They have bears?"

"Maybe."

"Let's go!"

Samir hopped out of his seat, the sugar from the milkshake working its giddy magic.

The circus was at the arena near the lake. As they got closer, Fouad scanned the horizon for a big blue tent.

"There it is. I see it," Samir said, pointing.

There it was. A big blue tent the same color as the cloudless sky, with a gold trim that stretched across the field. It was impressive.

Fouad parked the car, and they walked across the lot as the afternoon sun beat down on them. Despite the grand appearance of the tent, it was quiet; the crunch of gravel underneath their feet the only sound. There weren't many cars and no people milling around. They walked around to the back of the tent and found a teenager dozing in a fold-up chair, a tan baseball cap pulled low over his eyes. Fouad had to clear his throat to get the young man's attention. The attendant mumbled the price and slid two tickets across the table without Fouad ever seeing his face.

Inside the tent it was cool. Large fans whirred in the corners, rippling the blue cloth and giving the impression of being underwater. There were stands set up around the perimeter, selling food and offering games and rides, and a petting zoo with goats and sheep. A boy wearing a plastic firefighter's hat sat on a brown pony walking in slow circles, its head bowed. At the far end of the tent, a magician did card tricks for a handful of kids. There was some action everywhere Fouad looked, but it was all muted, like he was watching television with the sound off.

The quiet jarred him. He'd expected noise and activity. A teenage girl walked by carrying a bag of trash.

"Excuse me," he asked, "where's the clowns and the elephants? You know, the circus stuff?"

"The show starts at four o'clock," she said, without slowing her pace.

Fouad checked his watch. It wasn't yet three o'clock.

"How about we walk around for a bit?" he asked Samir. "What do you want to do?"

Samir looked around doubtfully, then sauntered over to the petting zoo. Fouad stood outside the fenced area and watched Samir kneel next to a sheep in repose, his fingers dancing over the animal's woolly fur. After a few timid pats, he began to stroke its back. When the animal tipped its head back towards Samir, a silent request for a head rub, Samir looked over at Fouad and grinned, his eyes electric. Fouad was struck by how much the boy looked like Fouad's own mother.

His family would be thrilled to learn of the boy's existence. Samir could make up for the disappointment Fouad had brought. They had tried hard to break through whatever was holding him, gently suggesting therapy and prayer, but he had shut them out. Wearied of their pleading, worried eyes, he had packed his things and left in the middle of the night. He drifted from place to place, picking up odd jobs. Eventually he ended up down south, as far away from them as he could get without falling into the water. In the brief euphoria following Samir's birth, Fouad had committed to getting sober and reuniting with his family, but the spiral pulled him back down to the bottom of the bottle. Samir would fit in with them in all the ways Fouad never could.

Samir walked back to his father. The sheep he'd been petting had fallen asleep.

"Want to play some games?" Fouad asked.

They stopped at all the game booths. Samir did several rounds of balloon shoot, trying to pop a balloon with a dart, but was unsuccessful. The woman working the booth gave him a lollipop anyway, which he pocketed. He played ping pong toss and duck pond, aiming a fishing rod into a bucket of water to hook a duck. He threw cabbages at a wooden clown's wide-open mouth, laughing when they hit the clown's head, which they did every time. He seemed unbothered that he lost every game until they got to the ring toss. Behind the table of glass bottles stood a wall of toys. After his third try, he stomped his foot.

"What's the matter?" Fouad asked.

Samir pointed at the toy wall.

"What?"

"The loggerhead sea turtle. I really want the loggerhead sea turtle."

Right in the center of all the garishly colored toys sat a subdued stuffed turtle.

"How do you know it's a loggerhead?" Fouad asked.

"Because it's brown and red on top and yellow on the sides. Loggerheads can weigh up to a thousand pounds, and they travel the whole world, farther than any other sea turtle." He held his hands out in front of him with his fingers splayed like he was waiting to catch a ball. His voice was awestruck.

Fouad smiled. His vision flickered to life—adult Samir holding the ratty stuffed turtle, telling his kids how his dad won it for him. He handed a dollar to the red-faced man running the booth and picked up a stack of rings.

"Let me see what I can do," he said, pretending to roll up his sleeves.

Samir bounced on his toes and clapped. Fouad threw a ring and it bounced off a bottle onto the floor. He shook off the loss.

"I'm a little rusty," he said. Samir laughed.

He tossed another and again it bounced. "Huh," he grunted.

He missed the third toss then paid for another round. He missed all three. He was sweating now and his jaw hurt from clenching his teeth. The spiral was tightening. He should walk away, but he couldn't. He had to win the turtle. He played three more rounds and missed them all.

"Come on pal, let somebody else have a turn," the red-faced man said after he'd picked up the fallen rings.

There were two kids standing behind them in line. A third stood off to the side, watching. Fouad threw down another dollar. The man scowled but laid down the rings. Again, Fouad lost.

"This game is rigged," Fouad said.

The man laughed. "It's fair," he said. "You just can't throw."

Fouad's mouth tightened.

"It's okay, Dad," Samir said.

Fouad set down another dollar. The man looked at it but didn't move to pick it up.

"You should listen to your kid," he mumbled.

"And you should shut your mouth," Fouad growled. His hands shook. A humming like a swarm of bees buzzed in his head.

181

"Alright, pal, move along. You're done here."

"No, I'm a paying customer. Give me the rings." He was shouting now.

"I said move along." The man motioned to the child standing behind Samir. "Come on kid, your turn."

"No, I'm not done yet," Fouad screamed. He slammed his fist on the table. The man ignored him, taking the child's money. "No," Fouad said. He hopped over the table and made for the toy wall.

"Hey buddy, what the hell are you doing? You can't do that," the man shouted.

Fouad snatched the turtle off the wall and threw it to Samir, who didn't move to catch it. "Hey kids, don't waste your money. Here." He grabbed toys in clusters and threw them over the table onto the ground. The adults around stared, their mouths open in horror, but one man laughed and gave Fouad a thumbs up.

The red-faced man pointed at Fouad. "You. Get outta here. I'm calling security."

"Yeah, who's that? The kid sleeping outside. Don't worry, I'll wake him up on my way out."

Fouad stalked out of the tent with Samir jogging behind him. He climbed into the truck and slammed the door. His breath came in ragged heaves. He opened the glove compartment and stared hard at the flask of whiskey, then slammed the drawer shut. Samir jumped and slid back in his seat. The turtle lay limp on the seat between them. Fouad tried to put the key in the ignition but his hands were too shaky. He dropped the keys in his lap and laid his head on the hot steering wheel. Before he could catch himself, he was crying.

"I'm sorry, son. I'm sorry," he wept.

He felt a hand on his back between his shoulder blades. Samir slid next to him and laid his head on his shoulder.

Fouad sat up. "I'm sorry, son. I'm—" He squeezed his eyes shut. "I'm not good, son. I have a problem."

Samir laid a finger on the scars on Fouad's arm. "Is this part of that problem?" he asked.

Fouad bobbed his head slowly.

Samir ran his fingertips across the scars, then covered them with his hand. Fouad wiped his eyes with the heel of his palms, overcome with fatigue.

"I should get you home," he said, starting up the truck.

Left would take them out of the arena, but Fouad turned right towards the lake instead. He crested a small hill and a panorama of water appeared. Samir sat up.

"Oh," he said.

"You've been here before, right?" Fouad asked.

"No, never."

"Really? Your mom never took you?"

Samir shook his head, his eyes on the water.

"You wanna check it out?" he asked.

"Can we?" Samir said.

Fouad parked and they walked over to the waterfront. From the top of the steps at the edge of the lake, they watched the water curl lazily along the shore. In the distance, a speedboat zipped across the lake. Seagulls floated down, their bellies skimming the water, causing it to ripple. Fouad breathed in the thick, humid air; closed his eyes against the mist that sprinkled his face when the waves came in. Samir tilted his face up to the sky, pointed, and smiled.

"We're still under the blue tent," he said.

"What?"

"The blue tent. Allah's blue tent."

Fouad studied the sky. Out there by the water, the sun washing his face, there was no spiral, and no vision either. He felt open, not outside of himself but comfortably within, not squeezed. He wondered, in all the times his thoughts had spun in endless circles, tossing around and crashing into each other, snatching him into their tightening whirls, why he had never thought to step outside. He laid his hand on top of his son's head and rubbed his hair, the thick coils bumpy beneath his fingers, like its own form of braille. Suddenly, a fish jumped out of the water, then fell back into the depths. Samir gasped.

"Daddy, did you see that?" he shrieked. Fouad laughed. "Look, look, it did it again!"

The fish jumped a third time, but before it could fall back into the water, a gull swooped down and scooped it into its beak. Samir squealed. "Oh, Daddy, did you see that?"

"Yeah, son, I saw it."

They sat and watched the water, not talking.

"You ever been fishing?" Fouad asked after a while.

"No."

Fouad thought of the loaded gun waiting for him on his dresser. His voice trembled. "Maybe—maybe I could take you sometime."

Samir smiled at him. "I think I'd like to do that."

Fouad dropped Samir off and headed home. He unlaced his boots and emptied his pockets onto the dresser. He picked up the gun and opened the chamber, shaking the bullets into his open palm, then slipped them back into their slots. Six bullets, one for each person in his life he'd hurt. He held the last one in his hand. One left, one not yet broken. He laid the gun back onto the dresser, the chamber gaping open, and placed the sixth bullet next to it. He might still do it. That last bullet might be the one that ended him. But first, he had to take his son fishing.

CHOTI
SABA GHAZI-AMEEN

This is the story of a girl. This is the story of how that girl found herself without even realizing she had been lost. This is my story.

It was the summer of 1976, and while parades were parading and freedom reigned in celebration of our nation's bicentennial, I was celebrating my own freedom.

I had just graduated kindergarten. I had made it through a whole year of full-day school. Dressed in my favorite patchwork overalls and rainbow striped shirt, I burst into the living room boldly exclaiming, "Ammi, Abbu, I'm free!" And really I was. It was the first day of summer, and time was mine. It was all mine.

I could barely contain myself as Mom stretched elastic around each of my braids. I pulled away and ran out the sliding door into the playground.

"Meera! Meera, where are you?" I ran to each one of the four playsets spread through the middle of our complex looking for my best friend until I found her, running right into her arms. We were both so excited we couldn't stop screaming, "We're free! We're free!"

With the newfound confidence only those who matriculate kindergarten possess, we claimed that playground. We slid down the slide… and dared to run up it backwards. We swung the swings as hard as we could so that they would wrap around the top bar and hang at precariously high heights that we had mastered. We buried ourselves in the sand pit, then broke free from its grip like the superheroes we were.

Oh yes, Meera and I dominated that space and barely an hour had passed.

It was time for the biggest challenge, the rope swing. Now, this swing hung from the middle of the bar and had a red disc at the bottom of a thick rope. It was impossible for any human to stand on it and balance as it teetered in every direction. But we were not ordinary humans. We were superheroes. We were the wonder twins. Why not take it up a notch and balance both of us.

First I stepped on, and as the disc tilted to the right, threatening to fling me, Meera gingerly stepped on and balanced the base. Grinning from the ease of our success, we began pumping, leaning back and forth and gaining momentum. My braids flew fiercely in the wind, mirroring the undaunted spirit bursting from my chest.

As the swing slowed down, we began spinning in circles, first slowly, then faster and faster. My hair flew up as we spiraled at dizzying speeds. Somehow, in the middle of all that fearless fun, my braid found its way into the rope, winding tightly around it until my check was pulled against the rough fibers, trapped.

"Meera, Meera, my hair is stuck!"

She jumped off the swing, leaving me teetering from right to left, all while trying not to move my head. Meera cocked her head to the side and said, "Yeah, its stuck. Wait. I'll go get some scissors."

The next part is a blur. I remember waiting and waiting as my eyes started to burn from holding back tears. I was a superhero. I was a wonder twin. I wasn't scared. I wasn't scared. I wasn't scared. It was probably minutes, but it felt like hours. I tried to look around to see where Meera was, but my head was locked to the rope at an awkward angle. I tried to run my fingers through the top of my braid and free it, but it wouldn't give. I saw a mother playing with her toddler in the sandbox and tried to call her for help, but only a hoarse whisper escaped my cracked lips. Hours and hours seemed to pass. My stomach hurt. And those darned tears started falling. I said the prayers I knew. *Bismillah, ar Rahman, ar Rahim.* Allah, please help me. I promise to be good. Please let go of my hair.

My feet were slipping off the ring, and my hands were getting sweaty holding the rope near my head.

I closed my eyes, and with one giant tug, I willed myself free.

I fell to the ground. I looked up at the swing and gasped. My braid, elastic intact, was hanging from the rope. I reached up to my head and felt the smooth spot where half my hair had been.

Blinded by my tears, mute from my dry throat, deaf from the throbbing in my ears, I stumbled into our courtyard. My mom came running to the sliding door, and by the look on her face, I knew it really was THAT BAD.

The doctor said it may never grow back, that the best bet was to shave my entire head, and that might stimulate new growth.

And so, age six, first summer out of school, I was bald. Keep in mind this was 1976. I was a rebel in my own right, but girls didn't shave their heads back then. There was no *Locks of Love* and no cool ways to hide the fact that I had no hair.

My parents, at a loss, took me to the department store to find a wig. Now, there were no kid-sized wigs in that era. The only wig the saleslady could find in extra-small was covered in curls. The hair was black, but that's where the similarity ended. My hair from my father was silky shiny and smooth. My hair from my mother was fierce with a life of its own, barely tamed by those braids she tied it into. Nowhere in my genetics was there the slightest trace of the curls that tumbled from that wig.

As I slipped on the scratchy cap, my jaw dropped at the site in the mirror. I looked like a middle-aged woman shrunken down into a kid's body. The tight curls didn't budge as I shook my head from side to side, but the cap, too loose for my head, slid around covering my right eye as I tilted left. "Don't worry, we have adhesive strips that will keep in in place," the saleslady assured my worried mom.

And then came the moment of truth. While school was out, Islamic school was ready to kick into high gear. I refused to go. "But Mom, everyone will wonder how my hair changed. What if the wig falls off? What if they laugh at me?" I sobbed on her shoulder. "I just want to be me again!"

I come from a family of five kids, and the nice thing about siblings is that they've got your back in times that matter. My younger twin brothers hugged me and told me I was pretty. My older sister grabbed my hand and said I could go sit in on her class if I wanted. My older brother offered to beat up anyone who bothered me.

So I made it to class. I guess my parents had a talk with the school because, miraculously, no one commented. Yeah, there was one boy who tried, but my brother solved that in a not-so-good-Muslim way we won't talk about here.

Then it happened. One day as we were driving to the *masjid*, I realized I had forgotten my wig! I begged my dad to go back, but we were too far already. I offered to sit in the car, said I would walk all the way back home. Anything! Just don't make me go to Islamic school like this.

By that point, my hair had reached a nice fuzzy state. I had a good quarter-inch covering my scalp. My little brothers said I looked pretty, and if I had a lollipop, I could pass as Kojak's daughter. My sister told me I looked cool. My big brother... well, he offered to beat up anyone who dared bother me.

And so I got out of the car, legs shaking, and made my way to the classroom. Too scared to look up, I slipped into my seat. And miracle of miracles, no one seemed to notice. One girl asked what happened to my pretty curls, but no one else so much as glanced at my head.

And I found out something that day. Head free from that scratchy wig and fake curls, brain thanking me for the release, I found out that I was still me. I was still Saba, the morning breeze from the east, the fearless fighter of summer freedom. I was still me. Kindergarten graduate, mud pie master. No bald spot, no wig, no fuzz-covered head changed that. I realized that my look doesn't define me. I am my own unique individual.

In the words of the oh-so-wise Dr. Seuss, "Why fit in when you were born to stand out?"

And if any of you have a problem with that, please see my older brother.

SIGHT: A SHORT STORY
ZAINAB FATIMA MIRZA

Prologue

Once upon a time, in a far-off land, there lived a group of One-Eyed people. They were kind and hard-working, and were often interested in helping other people. They were proud, not only of themselves but also of their land, for they had spent many years cultivating and growing it. The One-Eyed people were experts in hunting birds; the single eye on each of their foreheads helped them focus diligently when aiming at their prey. Trading these birds for wool with people from other lands was their livelihood, and so hunting them was a necessary job.

Over time the One-Eyed people became powerful and important and came to believe that their land was sacred, and they—with it—were blessed by God. In honour of their success and power, they decided to celebrate their achievements and their land once every month. On one special day every month they considered it tradition to eat and serve each other bannock, a tasty bread that they consumed with freshly hunted and cooked bird. The One-Eyed people were very proud that they had created such a prosperous land, and they looked for every excuse to celebrate their accomplishments. Although they believed they were kind, they would not hesitate to hurt anyone that threatened their accomplishments or power.

Years passed, and the One-Eyed people came to experience fortune as well as adversity. Despite their success, they were not always immune to famine and hardship. While once most of them were capable of hunting birds, many had now chosen to pursue other interests, and as such, their trade suffered. Since they were no longer hunting enough birds to trade for wool, wool—which was a resource they relied on for clothing—became scarce. New clothing became a luxury rather than necessity. The One-Eyed people became worried for the state of their society, and decided that the only way to ensure the continuous growth and success of their land was to welcome people from other lands, people who could help them in hunting birds and trading with other communities for valuable resources like wool. The One-Eyed people became hopeful for a better tomorrow as their leader announced that they would be welcoming Two-Eyed people into their land, by promising them opportunity, wealth, and prosperity.

"We must mark this day as a holiday, to celebrate this new change in our land," they remarked to each other.

"Let us all look to new and fruitful beginnings!"

Chapter 1

"But why do we have to leave?"

My mother turned to give me a warning look, as if to say: *Don't upset your father.* "We're only thinking of your future," she offered.

We stood at the edge of the harbour, huddled closely together as the early morning breeze pierced through our clothing. It was a cool summer dawn, though the sun had not yet risen. In the gloomy darkness, all I could see were the shadows of our village in the distance. Save for the sounds of the calm waves of the water, there was a sharp stillness in the air as we waited for my father's friend Abna to join us.

It felt only like yesterday when news had reached us that the One-Eyed people were welcoming others into their land. No one had expected them to open their arms to foreigners, for they were a very proud and close-knit people. At first my father did not believe that the news was correct. "It's too good to be true," he exclaimed to my mother. "Why do they suddenly care for us? What do they get from helping us, from letting us into their land?" He was not wrong to ask. The One-Eyed people had, historically, only looked out for other One-Eyed people.

My mother, ever the voice of reason, encouraged my father to be more open-minded. "But what if it's true?" She countered. "What if we really can go there? We can finally be successful. We can be rich. We can be happy!" She glanced in my direction with longing and hope. "Muqawama can be happy!"

Following her gaze, my father looked towards me. His brown

eyes softened when he looked at me, but nevertheless, a frown slowly formed onto his face, and he shook his head in confusion. "Why can't we be happy here?" He almost shouted.

It was true. Why couldn't we be? I was not invited to take part in their conversation, but as I sat on my sleeping mat in the corner of the room and listened to them argue, I could not help but wonder what life would be like in the One-Eyed people's land. They were successful and powerful people. It was well known that whenever a person went and settled there, they eventually assumed wealthy and comfortable lives. We did not have that same wealth and comfort here, nor did we have opportunities to attain it, but we made do with what we had. Was it not enough? Why couldn't we be happy with what we had?

I wondered what the One-Eyed people would be like, what their homes would be like. I felt both anxiety and excitement in the pit of my stomach as I thought about going to their land. Was it like ours? Did their trees sway to the music of the wind as they did here? Was their earth as rich as ours? Did they even think about any of this? Did it matter, when they had more important things to think about, like their wealth? A part of me prayed that my father would decide to take us to their land so we, too, could think about wealth instead of the earth, but the other part of me felt fearful of all that I did not know about them, or their land.

In the end, of course, it did not matter what I personally prayed for. My father had already decided that we would try our luck with the One-Eyed people.

Now we stood by the harbour, waiting for Abna to take us to Sight, the land of the One-Eyed people. He was my father's friend, as well as an ambassador for Sight's government, and so we had placed all our trust in his hands. He had promised to take us to Sight by boat, and had ensured us that we would reach there safely.

I could see the sun coming up slowly as we stood there waiting, and as sunlight penetrated our surroundings, the air seemed to come to life. Suddenly I could hear birds chirping and the flutter of wings as they flew above us. The air seemed abuzz with music, and the movement of the birds seemed like a dance, as the intangible feeling of hope grew on us heavily.

Maybe it won't be so bad, I thought to myself. Maybe I'll finally be free, like the birds, when I reach Sight.

Chapter 2

I had never thought of myself as different or strange until I reached Sight. I had always known that the One-Eyed people were powerful, but I had not realized that their power rested so much in their appearance. After I reached Sight, though, I became painfully aware that I looked different, that I was different from them.

As soon as we had reached the shores of Sight, there were a couple of One-Eyeds waiting to receive us. They stood on a wooden pier, and behind them I could see an empty large green field. The sky was clear, and the sun was shining, and seemed to kiss the field with its rays.

"Welcome to Sight," the woman exclaimed as we stepped out of the boat that was now positioned by the pier. We approached her slowly, warily and unsure of our surroundings. She was rather tall and large, and wore a simple white dress. She trained her eye on us and smiled, gesturing to our surroundings. "This beautiful land is now yours as well. We hope you can adapt into our society, and that sooner or later you see yourself as One-Eyed!"

My parents glanced at each other shyly. We had no idea what the woman was saying to us and had to wait for Abna to translate her speech. As soon as they understood what she had said, their faces brightened. Though we were exhausted from our long journey, looking at them now, one would not be able to tell that they were so worn. They turned to beam at me. "Hear that, Muqawama? We are One-Eyed now!" My father grinned.

I frowned and reached up to feel my face. As far as I could tell, I was still Two-Eyed.

The woman continued to chatter, and Abna translated her speech quickly so we could understand: "My name is Fally, and my partner here is Osmo. We're going to help you adjust to our land as brand new One-Eyeds. It is important that you understand the laws and customs of Sight, to ensure that you assimilate into our community well."

My parents nodded along and mumbled agreement, but I initially kept silent. I couldn't understand how I had become One-Eyed simply by entering Sight. Was I not allowed to be Two-Eyed in this land?

Slowly, timidly, I spoke up. "But we're Two-Eyed," I all but whispered, pointing at my face.

My parents turned to look at me sharply, and Abna hesitated, then shrugged in indifference and translated what I said.

We still hadn't moved from the pier, and the way Osmo placed his eye on me, a part of me suddenly feared that he would put us back on the boat and force us to return to our land. Instead he laughed lightly. "Of course you are." He responded slowly. "We look forward to your unique contribution to our society as Two-Eyeds, but hope that in time you will come to see yourself as One-Eyeds."

As Abna translated, my parents glared at me as if to command me to keep quiet. I winced and silently nodded, showing my agreement with Osmo's response.

We began to move away from the pier and towards the field ahead of us. I walked behind everyone, but as they moved ahead, my mother stepped in line with me and put her mouth near my left ear. "Don't upset them, Muqawama," she whispered.

Chapter 3

In the beginning it was lonely and difficult. Fally and Osmo placed us in a One-Eyed neighbourhood. Our hut was small and bare, but it was large enough for my parents and me to live in comfortably. After Abna, Fally, and Osmo left us to settle into the hut, I roamed through the two small rooms in my new house. There was nothing to see, really. It was up to us to buy sleeping mats and other necessities. The walls and floor were bare and the same wheat colour, except for the living area, where the floor was covered by a large black rug.

In my mind I could see my old home: it hadn't been much better than this hut, but it held many memories, our laughter, our hopes and dreams. It was where I had grown up. Every nook and crook held meaning to me. A crack in the wall of my room would mean nothing to a stranger, but to me it was a reminder of when I had once accidently thrown a rock at the wall while playing a game of toss.

This hut I stood in now was a stranger to me. I did not recognize the cracks or holes in the walls, nor did the space speak to me. I felt like an intruder in my new house.

"So." My father put his hands on his hips and glanced around the sitting area. "This is home now."

Was it? We may have had a place to live in, but could we really call this land ours? Was it as simple as that?

As time proved to us, home was not a place that would come easily to us in this land.

Sight, of course, was a beautiful place. If one walked out into one of the forests, it could easily be mistaken for a forest back home. The trees were luscious and green, the surrounding ground home for creatures of all kinds. I often spotted rabbits hopping around like I did in the forests back home.

Nevertheless, this was not enough to make Sight home for me. The One-Eyeds in our neighborhood were curious and kind, albeit aloof. Perhaps that was because of the language barrier between us, or perhaps it was because they did not know what to make of us. Although we had heard that they wanted to welcome foreigners into their land, I was no longer sure if that was truly the case. Sure, people like Fally and Osmo were very welcoming, but it seemed that our neighbours were not that happy that we were here.

We had one neighbour, Grei, who sat outside his hut every morning as my father passed by to work. By that time, we had learned some of their language, so when I waved goodbye to my father on the steps outside of our hut, I could understand Grei as he yelled at my father when he walked past.

"Hey, you! How do you like my job?" Grei sneered. "Are you happy, stealing jobs from good people?"

My father always ignored him and quickly walked away, hoping to avoid trouble. I, on the other hand, stood there feeling confused. Why did Grei feel that my father had taken his job?

My father had been hired as a hunter, whose main job was to hunt for birds. His employers felt that his two eyes would be an advantage when looking for prey. They were in dire need of good hunters, and hoped that my father would prove to be one.

The next time Grei yelled his profanities at my father, another neighbour who lived across from us was also standing outside. She clucked her tongue in disapproval at Grei when he started his usual tirade, and crossed the road towards me.

"Don't take him seriously," she comforted me as she came close. "He's just upset that he can't keep a job. The word is, he's such a bad hunter that he always gets himself fired in less than a week."

I did not comprehend all of what she said to me, but I understood the gist. I nodded at the woman and she smiled in response.

"My name is Ola. What's yours?"

I pointed at myself. "Muqawama."

And that was the start of a new friendship.

Chapter 4

For a short period, we were some of the only Two-Eyed families in Sight. Ola told me that Sight's government had been trying for some time to encourage more foreigners into their land.

"Slowly, outsiders are realizing that it is such a great privilege to live here," she told me one day, as we introduced a new Two-Eyed family into our neighbourhood. "Hopefully they can use their two eyes to help us grow as a society."

She was right. Before we knew it, there were hundreds of Two-Eyed families moving to Sight. The government of Sight had established that Two-Eyed people were very good hunters, and that their two eyes gave them an advantage in finding prey that One-Eyed people did not seem to have. They offered many Two-Eyed people hunting jobs on arrival to Sight, and so many Two-Eyeds accepted the offer.

Everything seemed to be going well for both groups of people. Although there were a few people like Grei who antagonized the Two-Eyeds, the majority appeared to welcome change and accepted that Two-Eyed people helped their communities grow and prosper.

Chapter 5

I don't know when exactly things started to change. Perhaps change was slowly happening around us the whole time but I did not know.

I do know that on one hot summer day, a fight broke out. To this day, I don't know why the fight escalated the way it did. Maybe it was because of the temperature. Everybody was sweating and on edge because of the blinding heat. Nobody could think straight that day; the sunrays seemed to be melting our brains.

I was in the field with Ola, picking berries for dessert that night. Near the edge of the field were a few young men, loitering around the fruit-picking women.

Suddenly I heard shouting as a One-Eyed man and a Two-Eyed man from that crowd began hurling insults at each other:

"Two-Eyed freak! Stealing our jobs from us! How dare you use your disgusting eyes to look at my woman!"

"At least we're not useless, sitting on our arses and waiting for jobs to be handed to us!"

"You're filthy! You can't be trusted! God knows what you all use that second eye for!"

"I'm sure you'd like to know. Maybe if you had another eye, you'd actually find a bird to shoot! Maybe your girl wants to be with a strong young hunter instead of a lazy deadbeat like you!"

They broke into a fist-fight soon after that.

I couldn't believe my eyes, or my ears for that matter. The two continued to fight, and it so happened that the Two-Eyed man was stronger than his opponent. He beat the One-Eyed man to a pulp, only to be pulled away by his companions after a crowd of One-Eyed people began to gather around them.

"That's right!" he yelled at no one in particular as he was dragged from the crowd. "Don't mess with us!"

He ran off, perhaps thinking that he could escape the consequences of his actions, but as it turned out, not only would he come to pay the consequences for his actions, so would all the Two-Eyed people.

Chapter 6

The change afterwards was swift and cruel. I could no longer go to the market without encountering resentful One-Eyed people. Sometimes they only stared at me angrily; other times they vocalized their anger.

"If you want to live in our land, you live by our rules!"

"We were kind enough to let you in here, but we didn't expect this ungratefulness from you all! You don't belong here! Get out!"

"Violence is in your blood! Don't pollute our land with your filth!"

"We should have never let you all in!"

These were the times that I wished, with all my heart, that I could hide. I did not even know these people, and yet they had decided that I deserved their insults. I knew that if only I could hide one of my eyes, I could fit in. They would never know that I was different, and they would accept me as one of their own.

I came home from the market one day and ran directly to the fire pit. My parents weren't home, so I had the place to myself. I sat in front of the fire pit and slowly pushed my hand in to grab a fist full of ash.

I stared at the ash in my hand. Could this solve my problems? Could I hide my origins with this ash? I closed my eyes and began to aggressively rub my forehead with it, praying for a miracle. If I could hide my second eye with the ash, maybe the One-Eyed people would not be able to tell that I was not one of them. Maybe then I would stop feeling as worthless and dirty as the very ash I was using.

Chapter 7

Soon the very government that had welcomed us into Sight began to campaign against us. Government spokespersons went from neighbourhood to neighbourhood to remind One-Eyed people that we were the reason for all their problems.

"Our economy would be so much better if it weren't for the Two-Eyed families leeching off of us," they preached, shaking their heads in dismay.

"There are so many of them now. It's too dangerous."

"They didn't like that we threw that Two-Eyed monster into prison? He deserved it! This is our land, and if they hurt one of us, they hurt all of us."

"We can't let them take over Sight. Let us reclaim the land that is rightfully ours."

I remembered when, long ago, they had encouraged our arrival into their land. How times had changed.

I no longer left our hut alone. Everywhere I went I continued to be met with accusing stares, and at times, threatening blows. I felt that it was better for all of us if I simply didn't show myself. I often lay on my sleeping mat and wondered where it had all gone wrong. What had I done to hurt these people? Why did they hate me so much?

My parents were just as fearful as I was; I often heard my father cursing the Two-Eyed man who started it all. However, I wondered: One-Eyed men fought amongst themselves all the time; why must we all suffer because of one Two-Eyed man?

Amidst the volatile environment, we mused about our lives in our old home, in a land far from Sight. We had left that home. We had left all we had ever known in the hopes that we could build a new home in Sight. A better home.

But what did we have now?

Epilogue

So hot. It was so humid. When had I last felt heat like this? I could feel my clothes sticking to me, the sweat from my body acting as glue.

I opened my eyes slowly, trying to remember where I was.

I could see nothing, except...it was dark but I could vaguely see...I could see shadows. Shadows of bodies. People. Surrounding me. I tried to move my arm and found that I could barely move without hitting someone around me.

A moan escaped my lips as I remembered where I was.

Teaching Camp. Designed to contain and teach Two-Eyed people how to behave like decent beings, like One-Eyed people.

A tear slowly slid down my cheek as I thought of my state. This humid, cramped space. The smell of feces penetrated my nose, forcing its way into my mind. I was stuck. I was helpless. I couldn't escape.

I closed my eyes and tried to convince myself that I was somewhere else. Anywhere but here.

I pictured my parents. Our home. The clear blue sky. Beautiful green trees swaying to the melody of the wind. Large fields filled with berries ripe for picking.

I thought of Grei. He had always been so angry at my father. Was he happy now?

And what of Ola? My friend. Where was she now? Did she know where I was? Did she care?

All I had ever wanted was a home...whether it was in my land, or in Sight...all I had ever wanted was a place I could call my own, in which I could be accepted and loved for who I was.

I opened my eyes again. Was this prison all I would ever call home now?

I remembered my first day here. The guard had all but thrown me in here, and before walking out, peered down at me with contempt. Told me I should get comfortable. "You're going to be here a while," he had sneered. "This is your home now. Get used to it."

Long ago I had thought that birds were free, and I had longed to be like them. After I came to Sight, I realized that they were not free. Birds moved like they were free, but in fact they were only biding time. Time that didn't belong to them. Borrowed time...until they were hunted. Killed.

My wish had, nevertheless, come true. I was now like the birds that I had once admired.

Hunted.

And perhaps one day, killed.

HOME IN A COLORED LAND
TAYYABA SYED

I remember the first time I saw the ground blanketed in white. The snow seemed stiff and secure, but my shoes sank right through it. Immediately, chills ran up my lower limbs through my spine. I shivered and locked arms around myself. I looked up to see if I could find any familiarity in the sky. This sky looked like a reflection of the ground, white and fluffy. It didn't look like my sky, nor could I see my sun. I was confused as to why the sun of America was hiding and couldn't warm my bones like the sun of Pakistan. Why did I feel so different here?

My five-year-old self couldn't comprehend how I was going to call this my new home. It wasn't just the sky and ground that were white here, but so were the faces. I didn't see myself in them, in their eyes or hair or food or words. I felt like a complete misfit because I wasn't one of them.

"So, where are you from?"

This was the question that formed my identity in my formative years. Where *was* I from? As a young child, I would only identify myself as a Pakistani instead of a Muslim or American, because that's all I knew.

It would be another eight years before I could *officially* identify myself as an American. It didn't make much of a difference though. My citizenship didn't change the color of my skin or hair. I was still treated like an "other."

I needed to get around my otherness, though. I had to find a medium to connect with my classmates, to understand them and make them understand me. So, I turned to books. Whenever we had library hour in school, I felt like a kid in a candy store. There were so many titles to devour as a curious reader. However, I quickly noticed something missing in the books that I was reading: me. I never truly saw myself in these books. It was as if the pages were as white as the people around me. These books weren't a reflection of me either and validated my otherness even more.

Was that how the majority of children's literature was supposed to be in America: non-inclusive? Why was I being taught in school about the pilgrims who came as immigrants and refugees to this country, while feeling like such an outsider myself? How can we co-exist if we aren't accustomed to seeing the richness of our diversity? When was home going to feel like home? When would I feel American? When would I feel accepted?

As a mother, I see my children dealing with that same void and emptiness as I did. That mirror is still missing in the books they read and the imagery they see. So, I thought to myself, I can wait another few decades to see if there will be more kids' literature that includes every race, religion and culture living in this country, *or* I can start writing these books myself. If I wanted representation as a Muslim American, I'd have to start from what kids are reading at their most impressionable age.

My book *The Blessed Bananas: A Muslim Fable* was a wonderful by-product of this vision. I just came up with the story one night as I laid my kids to bed. My children, hearing familiar Muslim names and phrases, felt like they were a part of the story as little Muslims. But hearing it once was not enough for them. They made me repeat the story often and told me it should be made into a book. Why? I believe it was because they finally felt visible.

I then made it a mission to give every Muslim-American child that same sense of visibility. I don't want kids to question the sky or the ground or the books or the images they see as not their own. Therefore, for the last few years, I've been presenting *The Blessed Bananas* as a puppet show to kids all across America. The story portrays our universal qualities of kindness and generosity. I want every child that hears this story or reads my book to feel included, and most importantly, accepted. I want them to realize that books and stories are tools of the heart. They can make you feel anything, but what I truly want kids to feel is that they belong anywhere God places them. I want them to proudly identify themselves as Muslims, as Americans, as individuals who belong here and feel at home in this colored land.

AHMED AND THE CLOCK
WENDY DIAZ

There was a young boy, so witty and smart.
His name was Ahmed and he had a very big heart.
With skin caramel brown, he wore bright glasses.
He was known to be smart and pass all of his classes.

He loved all his subjects, especially science.
He looked up to his teachers for providing him guidance.
He had plans for inventing something useful one day.
He gathered tools and gadgets and kept dreaming away.

One night while working with circuits and wires,
Building with his hands what his imagination inspired,
From pieces of scrap, he put together a clock.
He listened intently and heard "tick, tock, tick, tock!"

"Awesome!" he thought, so proud of himself.
"I'll show my teachers what I've built all by myself!"
It was getting late. "I should go to bed," he thought,
So he drifted to sleep to the sound of his clock.

The following day as he hurried to school,
He put his clock in a box where he kept his tools.
Eagerly he rushed to his engineering class.
"I can show my invention to my teacher at last!"

But when Ahmed began, his teacher raised a brow,
"It's a clock," he explained, "and it works! I'll show you how!"
The teacher interrupted and didn't seem pleased.
"Keep it in your bag, where no one can see."

Ahmed was confused but did as he was told.
He continued the day with his clock in tow.
In English class, as the teacher taught,
Everything was quiet, except for a "tick tock, tick tock."

"What is that noise?" she asked, annoyed.
"It's just my clock," responded the young boy.
"Would you like to see it? I made it last night!"
As he opened his bag, the teacher's eyes opened wide.

"That looks like a bomb!" she cried out loud.
Ahmed understood his engineering teacher now.
But sadly, by then it was much too late.
The teacher told the principal what Ahmed had made.

"I think we should call the police," they discussed,
And before long, Ahmed found himself handcuffed.
The police officers asked him, "What is in this box?"
Ahmed answered, trembling, "It's just a clock."

Ahmed was scared; he could say nothing else.
"I just wanted to impress my teachers," he thought to himself.
"I couldn't hurt a fly. Why would they be suspicious?"
He was hurt and saddened by the principal's actions.

But this was the world in which Ahmed was living,
Where people had learned to not be forgiving.
They were fearful of things they didn't understand,
Like other races, beliefs and religions like Islam.

Ahmed and his family were of Muslim faith,
And despite being American, they faced racism and hate.
To some other people, all Muslims were suspicious.
They accused them of things that were often fictitious.

So what Ahmed had thought was a cool invention
Seemed to staff at his school like a possible weapon.
News of Ahmed's arrest spread far and wide.
Before long, many spoke out on his side.

#IStandwithAhmed their slogan became.
Soon Ahmed Mohamed was a household name.
Businessmen, celebrities, even the president spoke,
Reminding the world that there is still hope.

Ahmed was released, cleared of false accusations,
But not before his face was on every news station.
At his home, the press waited to hear him talk,
About the ordeal with his famous clock—tick tock, tick tock.

Since then he left school and made new plans.
He has a bright future and gained plenty of fans.
But the greatest lesson from his experience
Is never to judge based on beliefs or appearance.

No one should have to feel ashamed of who they are,
And all children should be allowed to reach for the stars.
Young Ahmed is just one of so many like him,
Full of hopes and aspirations, dreams and ambitions.

So we say, go on, young Ahmed, and never fear,
Those who will stand for you will always be near.
Keep striving and dreaming as all children should,
For the reward for good is nothing but good.

PART SEVEN: OCEAN OF HUMANITY

ODE TO TEA
TEHMINA KHAN

As I toss the crinkled
black leaves
into the kettle,
I watch your
golden amber hue
seep into
clear water
glowing like
the fossilized sap
that freezes an insect
in time
and adorns the neck of a queen.

When I sip
your steaming brew,
your heat spreads
to every cell of my body,
my senses awaken
and I can see
my people
across the ocean,
all sipping tea.

The bitter fragrance
tempered
by milk and sugar
or a drop of honey,
one golden liquid
melting into another,
to form a perfect balance
of bitter and sweet.
Less tyrannical than coffee,
less decadent than chocolate,
you are dreamworlds awakened,
pure sun in a cup.

The wine of great poetry
is nothing
compared to your humble brew
served in mud huts
and city slums,
in third class
train compartments
and fishing boats on
great rivers.
Served always
with a grace
worthy of kings.

Every morning,
every afternoon,
I sit and hold
a hot cup in my hands
and bring it to my lips
and share my drink
with every person in the world.

BOLD BREW
SABA GHAZI-AMEEN

coffee dark
strong brew of bold brown
don't dilute it
with vanilla cream

coffee dark
robust cup of caffeine
don't sweeten it
with bleached sugar

let columbus imbibe insipid intoxicants
hazy constellations stray his course

let radcliff sip pale blanched tea
pinkie raised shivering on his icy isle

come earth mother, blue sky, moon wolf
let's dance in my *haveli*
stomp out foreign borders
to the rhythm of our deep devotions

come muhammad, ai'sha, yusuf
lets rekindle our fires
roast unadulterated beans
grind the grounds of our fertile soil
spirit guides at our sides

yes rama, krishna, sita
let's smear red earth, wet henna on our hands
toast our ancient codes
drink the rich elixir of our heritage

let's fill our lungs with the vapor
of strong brown brew
and inhale that deep deep
coffee dark

WHEN I AM NOT HERE
@STUDENTASIM

Thought: When I am not here, I think about *Sadaqah Jaariyah**.
>Imagine perpetually helping people, even after you pass away,
through some means, actions, or devices that you either
developed or helped develop.

Imagine that stream of good deeds, for each living person you're
helping on earth, marching into your grave like soldiers rescuing
you from your evil sins, defeating each sin one at a time. What
would that feel like?

Thought: When I am not here, I remember being a student.

I admit it. I am a 'student.' It could sound a little strange to hear
someone who has been out of school for a long time identify
themselves as a student, but aren't we all students? And
everyone knows students are sinners: it takes time for them to
get it right, and even when they do, there's always something
new to learn. It is an endless loop of starting from the
beginning and coming to a certain point of understanding (*or
not*), all the while making many mistakes along the way.

I am okay with being a student, but alas, there are good students and
bad students. I could be a good one or bad one at different
times, but I am willing to take the journey. I am okay with being
the underdog. I am okay with not being the knower. I am okay
with making the mistakes. And I am okay with being desperate,
like all students are, but also desperately trying to make a
contribution.

Thought: When I am not here, I think about developing tools.

As a student, I think it would be great if I could develop tools, anything
of use, that could help another, now or in the future.

The great thing is there are so many options out there to develop
something useful: a book, a film, a playground, a water well, a

software application, a physical tool, a process, an organization, a social movement, new medication, even a small donation to help some project get off the ground. The list goes on and on. There's just so much that someone else can benefit from.

My wish? I think about the body of work I have developed: some books, films, prints, and the like. I wrote for the children. I wrote for the people. Could my work actually touch them and make a difference in their lives?

Thought: When I am not here, I think about my family.

How will they live? Will they be safe? What will they do? Will the kids know how to get out of trouble? How will they defend themselves? Will they learn other languages? Hate is on the rise, so how will they balance a second-generation Pakistani-Canadian identity living in Canada? Will they remember and speak Urdu? Will they remain Muslim? Will they visit Pakistan even though they were not born there? Their mother's grandparents live there, my parents lived there, and my grandparents died there. What will they do if they are out of work? Will the kids love each other and help each other? How will they better themselves? Will they constantly think about improvement? Will they forgive each other? Will the kids have families? Will they remember those many lessons I tried to show them? Will they remain students? Will they remember me? Will they pray for me?

Thought: When I am not here, I think about the children of the world.

So precious, so beautiful. Little angels that are such keen students, so innocent, so much potential. My work naturally gravitates towards them to try to equip them with mental ammunition for what's to come.

I think about the children in places like Pakistan every time I go back. Those innocent souls playing in the streets, even with very little, not knowing the world is waiting to corrupt them and drink their innocence.

I wish I could do so much for the children of the world, so much, so
much for the children of the world.
Inshallah...

Thought: When I am not here, I think about addiction.
That powerful thing, addiction, and we as a society struggle with it.
Many never get help. It's that silent killer of the mind, body,
and soul. Why weren't we taught formal skills to deal with
addiction while we were young and in school, before it became
a permanent guest inside us?
Addiction beheads dignity. It corrupts everything in its path. It makes
you an enemy of who you are. Why do we have to live with
this? How can we get away from it?

Thought: When I am not here, I think about the internet.
Agreed, it can be and is used for so much productivity. But I think
about the vices available online and how easily we slip
into them, because privately, the interaction is completely
unregulated to the heart's desire. That dirty imagery, those
naked bodies, the pictures, immoral conversations, greed, lust,
jealousy, the massive time loss, the proliferation of the human
desire to the *nth* degree.

Thought: When I am not here, I think about my parents.
Those two beautiful people who raised me. I am so grateful. So many
lessons, so much support. What would I have done without
them? I have thanked them in my book projects, which was the
least I could do in a formal way. A mercy and a blessing from
Allah, my parents.
I just learned that my good friend's father passed away, and *inshallah*,
I need to spend more time with my parents. They live literally
next door, but my life consumed me. My work consumed me. I
didn't call them for days. Repeat: They live next door...

Thought: When I am not here, I think about my neighbourhood street. The good neighbours and the not-so-good ones. I also think about all the people who speed, thinking residential streets are NASCAR speedways. I despise those people.

Thought: When I am not here, I think about my body. Those many days I did not train. Those many days I did not eat well. What I could have been. That body, it would have responded, but only if I made health a priority.

Thought: When I am not here, I think about the times I was late. The missed opportunities: jobs, relationships, prayers. Consistency was never in me. I could never win without it. It is something I would have to learn.

Thought: When I am not here, I think about society. Will it be more hateful? Or will people unite at some level? Will human behaviour be grisly, or can there be acceptance? Will divorce persist? Will the Family break down in different ways? Will our children be less and less tolerant? Will our every movement be surveilled? Will we still value faith? How will we work and earn? Will crime increase or decrease? Will there be more war and suffering? Can the world not be just? How will artificial intelligence interfere with just being human? Or are we destined to turn into something else as a species? Why can't we end world famine, hunger, and poverty? What is it about pride? What is it about the difference of opinions that has made our humanity at odds with itself? What is it about not getting along? Are we not nations and tribes that can get to know one another like the Qur'an states in 49:13? Are the best amongst us not the ones who have done the best deeds? Why do we harm our planet and wish it were dead?

Thought: When I am not here, I think about how much I didn't give.
The other day, an older lady was pushing her walker in the parking lot.
As I drove by, I slowed down because she was on the roadway
near the curb. We both smiled at each other at the same time,
and I raised my hand and waved, and she raised her hand and
waved. It was a beautiful moment. But I didn't stop.
As I drove past her, I immediately felt I should have stopped. I was
with someone, and I asked them if I should turn around to see
if the lady needed help, and they said, "No, no, she'll be fine."
But I still didn't accept that reply in my heart. Why didn't I just
turn around?

Thought: When I am not here, I think about my desires.
I never knew who I was. I lost almost all of my potential by giving into
my desires. I could have put all that potential into myself if I
had just said NO, and I could have used it to transform myself
into an indivisible force.

Thought: When I am not here, I think about courage.
I talked a lot about courage, and thought a lot about courage, but
I wasn't courageous enough. I admit, as time went on, my
courage did improve compared to when I was a child, but
nonetheless, it wasn't where I wanted it to be. I know I could
have actively improved my courage, and this did occur to me,
but then why didn't I develop it? The moments stripped me
each and every single time, and it still wasn't enough?

Thought: When I am not here, I think about my life.
That I was a sinner. Not that I am making excuses, but it's just a fact.
That there are some who cannot forgive me even after I have
apologized. Why did I make those MISTAKES? WHY?!
Ignorance was my enemy. I should have known better. Why
wasn't I effective enough? I did try a little. I did try to take
some steps. But I fell short. Why didn't I do more? I know I
missed a lot of prayers. I lacked experience. I was arrogant. I

know. So much time bled through. Why did I go wrong? Some know they'll make it to Heaven. They are just so sure! I was always that D- kind of player in life in everything anyway. And getting a D- on the Day of Judgement would be acing the test of life... because you passed! You made it to Heaven! WOOH! The Promised Land! But over here, the final mark, a D-? Only Allah knows best... and I beg Allah to remember me, that I was a student, that I knew I fell short... but there were some moments in there I really tried so hard for you...

Thought: When I am not here, ...

Thought: When I am not here, ...

Thought: When I am not here, ...

Thought: When I am not here, ...

Thought: When I am not here, ...

Thought: When I am not here, ...

Thought: But I *am* here, ...

* *Sadaqah means charity. Jaariyah means continuous. Sadaqah Jaariyah is ongoing charitable acts that may be reaped even long after one has passed away. In a continuous flow, these acts bring benefit to the receivers (who in turn may benefit others), while also bringing continuous blessings to the giver.*

PASSION
TEHMINA KHAN

From the plains of southern Africa,
our ancestors set out on a quest for passion.
This source of all stories
brings us a billion nests of compassion.

You begged our parents for stories –
for the songs of beloveds long gone.
Now spirit voices embrace you,
as you emerge dressed in compassion.

Our mother tells my son,
"Before you were born you were a star in the sky."
He gazes into the sparkling night
at that spilled treasure chest of passion.

On my wedding day, I held my beloved's hand
and waited for our grandmother,
but she was gone, her laughter buried,
the air bereft of her passion.

Remember – you are no predatory cat.
Our bipedal bodies move three miles per hour.
So throw away your wristwatch,
and travel at the speed best for compassion.

The roses and lilies have gathered
amongst the dandelions and wild grass.
Tomorrow they'll wither and become
the detritus left of this passion.

The city in which you love him lies on the Hayward Fault,
where plates collide.
Mountains rise in geologic time.
Evidence of the Earth's zest for passion?

Majnoon dressed in rags
still wanders in the desert shouting *Laila!*
She doesn't hear him.
Where are you God? Is this your best compassion?

Our African tribe multiplied, divided,
then multiplied over peak and plain.
So destroy all weapons before we aim them,
possessed by our passion.

Forty-three years ago our parents
promised each other an unknown journey.
Now they've handed us the keys to their city –
an open fortress of compassion.

Tonight, dear one, the devil and the angels
have tossed their scorecards away.
Let them dance through your muscles now
as passion suggests compassion.

O Usmi, don't you see?
Apy is trying to shelter you in a house of words.
Go then with your beloved.
Build your own house at the crest of passion and compassion.

CONSTELLATIONS
SABA GHAZI-AMEEN

daughter of ansar
yathrib's blood courses through my veins
pumping through my heart's chambers
echoing my beloved mustafa's name

prophet to the people
mercy to the worlds
guide to the revelations
soother of searching souls

thousands of years may separate us
the light of your spirit shines on
in the constellations of the *sahabiyaat*'s stories
illuminating your presence in this world and beyond

i look to the mothers of believers
the dauntless daughters and sisters of our souls
the steadfast and loving women
who made sure your message was told

and so, by the sky that is raised above us
i send blessings on baraka, your second mother
excited, she ecstatically exclaimed, "dear amina! your baby is a blessing
who will light these desert mounts in glorious wonder"

blessings upon blessings
baraka was a constant on your voyage
steadfast through trials and tribulations
she was among of the first to embrace your message

and by the mountains that are set firmly
i send my love to khadijah, your beloved partner
older yet unfazed, she proposed to you
upon witnessing your brilliance and pure honor

shaking when the revelation was squeezed from you
khadijah comforted you in the sanctuary of her embrace
even as you doubted your purpose
she stood solid with confidence and grace

she knew the divine could never abandon you
after all you are as sadiq and al amin
she knew your search for the pure truth
would lead you to the path of the righteous *deen*

by the thunder that declares allah's glory
may dear aisha be showered in light
feisty, brilliant and loving
she was the one who was your greatest delight

outrunning you in races of humor and wit
adoringly sipping water from the very same glass
she asked, " rasul, how much do you love me?"
you smiled, "like a binding knot, that will always last"

known for her intelligence, integrity and grit
you made her your greatest trustee
declaring, "half the faith rests with aisha"
she reported over 2000 of your *hadith*

and by the thunder that declares the divine's glory
i send peace to your brave umm salama
immigrating twice, weathering perilous journeys
fighting battles beside you for allah *subhanahu wa ta'ala*

like you she was known for her speaking
beautiful language, expressed with pure clarity
a scholar, a feminist, an orator—umm salama
made sure women were treated equally

she asked why the qur'an did not mention women
then heard you reciting a revelation soon after
stating there is no favor among the sexes
devotion to allah is the only elevating factor

by the olives, date palms and grapes that grow
upon sweet safiya i send *dhikr* and prayer
a jew who surrendered her soul to islam
taking you as her husband and protector

the beauty of the revelation made her weep
focused, she studied and learned jurisprudence
defending women and the voiceless
from anyone who tried to misconstrue it

and by the earth that is spread across the horizon
prayers for fatima, your devoted daughter
a face like yours, shining bright as the moon
she modelled a simple life like her father

she cried in elation accepting your message
stood ready to be your human shield
shoving away anyone who tried to hurt you
nursing your wounds on the front lines of the battlefield

as you lay on your deathbed and whispered to her
she sobbed when you said it was your time
then smiled when you told her the news
that she would be joining you in a very short time

by the qur'an and all that is beautiful
i look to my sisters who knew my rasul
women with qualities and attributes he admired
show me what he held dear and true

my love for my prophet runs deep
the best of allah's creations
balanced, loving, playful, devoted
a source of the *ummah*'s admiration

my sasul glowed like the moon
my nabi shone like the sun
an ansar—my heart will always harbor him
up until the hour its final beating is done

THE VIRGIN & THE UNICORN, A TALE OF MANHOOD, MYTH, MYSTICISM & POTENTIAL MURDER
ZAINAB BINT YOUNUS

Once upon a time, in what was once known as the New World—the name itself was uttered with a combination of scandal and intrigue, contemptuousness and envy—but what is now merely known as 'America' (and this name is uttered in tones of fear and anger, with all the bitterness of those whose lives were shattered in pursuit of "the American dream"), there lived a young man who appeared most unremarkable and yet, as we will come to see, was not quite so unremarkable after all.

He was reckoned a boy, still, for the New World had a strange habit of denying the blossoming of its youth; in truth, he was very much a young man. In the Old World, he would have been expected, at this age, to be at the very least an apprentice to a smith or a squire to a knight or even a fisherman already providing for a wife whose belly was swollen with their first child.

But he lived in the New World, and so this man-boy lived according to the standards of this world, and though his skin was honey-dark and his eyes amber-bright and his beard already grown in, a proud lion's-mane, he had no wife. Rather, he lived with his mother in a small, cramped set of rooms called an 'apartment'—a far cry from the sumptuous suites known as apartments in the Old World, where even a young man of our young man's age would have already begun collecting his harem, guarding them protectively within the sprawling villa where no male had access save the master himself and his own sons.

Our young man, as we said, had no wife and no harem. This would be shocking in the Old World, but in the New World was not; what was shocking, however, even by the New World's standards, was that he was a virgin.

His name, that we may become better acquainted with him, was Musa Alvarez.

Virginity has always had power of its own: the tears of a virgin are a vital ingredient of any reliable truth serum; a virgin's innocence is one of the few things that may compel creatures of the Unseen to reveal themselves;

the essence of a virgin's first kiss may either break a curse or seal it for all eternity. In Paradise, maidenly virgins await the Hereafter, eternally loyal to their husbands-to-be; there, too, reside chaste youths who will serve the believing women with chalices of glimmering drinks, their countenances bright as pearls. Virginity has always been a weapon and a prize, the most dangerous tool and the sweetest temptation by virtue of its most delicate state.

Alas, all of this has been forgotten by most in the New World; indeed, even the Old World has lost its veneration for virginity, both male and female, and all that remains is a twisted sense of possessiveness over the sexual purity of its daughters, while turning a blind eye to the immoral indiscretions of its sons. They do not realize that every act of illicit carnality strips them of their own strength, that their own masculinity is sacrificed by acting upon heedless lusts. But so it has become—the power of innocence has been lost, and so power itself is hidden from those who seek it most fervently.

Musa Alvarez lived in a city of palm trees and a bay of water crowned by a glittering bridge; a desert colonized by silicon technology and sleek chrome buildings, built upon ancient burial grounds and wresting more than one creature of sand and flame from its home, leaving them clinging to shadowy back alleys and long stretches of highway.

And in this city of buried fire and ripening dates lived someone else—well, many someone else's, but this someone else matters to our story—and she was much, much older than our youthful hero, though she did not look it. Being the daughter of a *ghulaam* father from Paradise (though he had chosen to foreswear eternal youth, that he may enjoy the full privileges of maturity), and of a very daring *jinniyyah* mother, gave her both an impressive lifespan and a particularly unique set of genetics.

Zumurrud's eyes were lustrous as onyx, her complexion both pearlescent and suffused with inner flame, but she was not, all things considered, considered particularly beautiful by the standards of her maternal tribe, nor did she exude the air of ethereal serenity that was the hallmark of her father's people.

She was also short-tempered, given to flights of fancy, and had an unhealthy fascination with the Sons of Adam and Daughters of Eve. Her mother had long ago eschewed the earthly realms and its vagaries for the tranquil ether of the Seven Heavens, and her daughter's insistence on mingling, however invisibly, amongst the People of Clay disturbed her. It was not that she was wont to commit the crime of *Iblees* and claim superiority of the *Jinn* over humankind, but Zumurrud's mother was uncomfortably reminded of her own adventurous indiscretions prior to her pious reformation and settlement into marital bliss (not necessarily in that order).

In any case, Zumurrud found herself drawn to those places which held echoes of the Old World of her people, even in the urban jungles of the inner city. It was there, in a patch of scrub and prickly succulents and tiny glowing embers of sand that held a thousand secrets, surrounded by buildings of raw cement and peeling paint, barbed wire and the bitter incense of smog and sand-musk, that Zumurrud met Musa.

Inevitably, unavoidably, with the definitive certainty of *naseeb* and the too-neat, too-predictable symmetry of a thousand and one love stories, she fell hopelessly, maddeningly in love with him.

You must know that the many tribes of the *Jinn* have been given talents and gifts, skills and tools unique to them, just as every nation amongst humans boasts of its own abilities and technologies. Zumurrud's mother hailed from an ancient tribe of smokeless fire and the ability to step betwixt and between, to veil themselves in shadow or shimmer into visibility, to see—even if only in wisps—auras of power and fear and joy and lust and love.

Virginity, as you may recall from our previous soliloquy, is a powerful thing; all the more so when it is cultivated and guarded carefully, protected from onslaughts of seduction. For as the Prophet had said, such nobility and strength and purity deserved nothing less than the shade of the One God's throne on the Day of Judgment.

In the courtyard, Musa Alvarez sat back onto his prayer mat, brow furrowed. Today had been difficult, a struggle to maintain his refusal to join the mindless violence—and guaranteed protection—of the local street gangs. He had promised his mother, and himself, that he would not allow himself to be swept up into the temptation of a fraternity founded on crime and fraught with the promise of a rap sheet before entering college. The greatest battle he fought, however, was not sidestepping fistfights and territory tagging, but avoiding the shy smiles and unsubtle flirtations of the young women who competed for the affections of unavailable males. It was, perhaps, rather trite, but as a red-blooded young man, it was difficult to deny or ignore the effects of silky hair tossed over bared shoulders, or long-lashed eyes casting inviting glances towards shadowy corners. Musa had so far resisted the illicit charms of cheerleaders and chess club alike, but it was becoming increasingly difficult as prom loomed ever closer.

One particular upperclasswoman, a doe-eyed, red-haired vixen, had brushed against him in the hallway, smirked at his jump backwards, his cheeks burning, and said saucily, "I heard that your religion lets you have four wives... why have one prom date when you could have three more? Three other girls tagging along with us sounds pretty exciting to me." She winked at him and sashayed away, leaving him with thoughts that—later, after he frantically referred to his trusted *fatwah* website— he was relieved to learn he was not alone in having questions about the intimate permissibilities of polygamy in Islam.

Wracked with both guilt and desire, Musa wondered how much longer he would be able to uphold his vows of chastity.

More and more often, he would retire after school to the courtyard of his apartment complex. It was a coarse kind of place, as prickly and dry as the rest of the city, but he liked its harsh comforts and the solitude it offered him. No one liked coming to this isolated square of sand and dust and stunted cacti; there was far more excitement to be had in more dangerous areas. Some days, Musa buried himself furiously in his books, determined to maintain the GPA he needed for the scholarship that would take him far from the only neighborhood he had ever known. Other days, like today, he needed to expend brute physical energy. One hundred and twenty-seven push-ups in, he finally collapsed, rolling onto his back and heaving as his muscles shook from his efforts. Sweat streamed down his face and into his beard, small rivulets cutting through the dust. Though his body was exhausted, his mind finally felt clear; he winced in embarrassment at the thoughts he had been fighting off all day.

"Oh, don't stop yet—just three more to round it up to one hundred and thirty." The voice was low, husky, and distinctly feminine.

Musa bolted upright and whipped around. He saw no one.

And then he did.

Out of the long, lazy shadow of the sole palm tree in the courtyard, stepped... a shadow? Or what began as a shadow, only to slowly undulate into solid form: scraps of sunspots, a penumbra unfolding, gathered, darkened, and blazed—a complexion as sun-burnt as his own, but glowing almost pearlescent; eyes that flickered with literal flame, dancing with wicked humour; lithe limbs enrobed in a darkness that rippled in the nonexistent breeze. The figure that stood before him now was as feminine as the voice that had preceded it.

"A'uthu billaahi min ash-shaytaan ar-rajeem!" The words came unbidden to Musa, an instinct both spiritual and survivalist, recognizing that what his eyes beheld was both preternatural and supernatural, something against which only Divine Protection would defend.

The glowing eyes narrowed, the coral-red mouth losing its mischievous curve and pursing instead. "I'm not the devil," she said tartly. "I may have been borne of smokeless flame, but so too have I tasted the rivers of milk and honey... from my father's own chalice, may I add."

Musa's eyes narrowed in turn. "You're a *jinn*."

She flicked an ember at him from her fingertips, and it landed in his beard, sizzled for a moment, and went out. "You needn't sound so suspicious," she chided. "Yes, I am, of a kind. No, I am not here to possess you," she snapped, in answer to his unspoken thought. "You may call me Zumurrud. I shall call you... Lionbeard." She smirked at his expression, his consternation at this sudden, unasked-for familiarity.

"Not much of a conversationalist, are you?" she commented,

circling him. She gave him the impression of a lazy she-cat, only a little hungry, but dangerously playful. "Pity, you sound so much more clever when you write your little poems. Ah, well, perhaps you are more the strong, silent type." She glanced at him sidelong, her eyes lingering on the still-gleaming muscle of his bicep.

"Are you trying to seduce me?" Musa asked flatly. This already felt all too familiar—the coy teasing, the brazen glances. His irritation overcame his stupefaction at the supernatural, and he frowned at the shadow-woman.

Zumurrud reared back, offended. "No!" Then she paused, the corner of her mouth curving into a guilty smile. "Perhaps a little," she admitted. "But you make it hard not to, Lionbeard." Her gaze raked over him, lingering appreciatively on the feature she so clearly admired.

"Lower your gaze," he said shortly.

Her grin widened. "Well, if you insist..."

"Not like that!"

She pouted. "It's rude to retract the invitation."

His frown deepened. "Are you even Muslim?"

Now she looked genuinely insulted. "Of course I am. Don't tell me you're just another brown boy who dismisses every *jinn* as an evil demon. Have you ever even read *"Surah al-Jinn?"* Or is *The Arabian Nights* and *masjid* aunty stories your only source of information on my kind?"

"You just admitted to attempting to seduce me," he pointed out. "It does seem in keeping with the nature of the tales told about your people."

"Only a little," she objected. "And being Muslim doesn't render me blind. Or immune to certain... needs."

He laughed bitterly. "You're telling me."

She rolled her eyes. "Come back to me when you've been celibate for a few hundred years, not just a couple decades. The Muslim marriage crisis isn't limited by species, you know."

"A... few hundred years?"

She preened. "I do look good for my age, I know." Musa ran his fingers through his beard, shaking his head. He was not quite sure whether he believed what was happening—if he was, in fact, being flirted with by a girl who had materialized out of shadow, a *jinniyyah* who quoted Qur'an and gave him a nickname, who casually claimed to be hundreds of years old, whose eyes glinted silver and stygian as she watched him.

Zumurrud inhaled sharply as she observed the flicker and flame of lust and loneliness, conviction and confusion, piety and purity—a faded fire compared to the one that burned around the edges of her own shadow-nature, but his blazed with a clarity that was utterly human and yet something other, too.

"Do you know," she said quietly, "why women are drawn to you so?"

Musa's smile was sardonic. "Because of my dazzling good looks?" He gestured dismissively. "It's all a game for them. Tempt the straight edge boy at school, see who he finally gives in to—it's an ego trip, that's all."

She shook her head, dark tendrils wrapping around her closely. "No. That's not all. Although yes, you are quite handsome—believe me, I've been around long enough to develop excellent taste in men—but there is something else. There is something about you that calls to us, something in your nature that is different and rare and precious." She cocked her head. "Have you ever heard of the tale of the virgin and the unicorn?"

Musa looked puzzled. "What?" Zumurrud's expression was wistful and longing at once.

"Long ago, when maidens were many and both the *buraq* and its cousins wandered the deserts and forests of Old World and New World alike, those who sought rare ingredients for alchemy, or simply the thrill of the hunt, knew that there was only one way to lure their ethereal equine prey.

"The most effective and valuable of bait is a virgin. Not cranky bachelors or sarcastic spinsters—well, they would do in a pinch, but it was always a prickly affair—but young men and women in the prime of beauty and desire, lustful and longed-for, who still held their chastity for love of God and honour.

"Take a virgin to a desert oasis or a meadow in the forest, and there you have the perfect trap for a unicorn. No creature fashioned from the ethereal can resist the call of such purity. Like calls to like, and so long as a son of Adam or daughter of Eve abstains from the pleasures of the flesh, the *buraq* and its kind will seek to bask in the pleasure of that innocence.

"The alchemists, the artists, even the *ulemaa*, all had their reasons for obtaining the flesh, blood, or tears of a unicorn. And so they would seek a virgin, male or female, all unknowing, and spin them a tale or pay them a fee for some minor service, whilst the truth of the plot was hidden from them. Then—in the silence and solitude of that oasis, that meadow, that valley-between-the-worlds—the virgin and the unicorn would behold one another, both caught in the splendor of the other, their hearts quivering. And then the hunter would strike, the creature captured, and the virgin's innocence lost in a way far beyond the physical.

"You see, it was both the purity and the pain of both virgin and unicorn which lent power to the ingredients which every alchemist sought."

"I don't get it." Musa's voice cut through the lilting, lyrical words that the *jinniyyah*'s voice spun, the sand-visions dancing before them, spiraling away into the dust. "What's the point of telling me all this?"

Zumurrud's eyes flared in annoyance. "The point of this," she snapped at him, "is to tell you that you, Lionbeard, are both virgin and unicorn, and so you are desired in more ways than one." Her voice softened, deepening with raw vulnerability and hunger for something unspeakable.

"I have fallen in love with you, Musa Alvarez, and I have been commanded to kill you."

ALLAH O AKBAR!
SALMA ARASTU

It is the call to my prayers
Allah O Akbar, Allah O Akbar, Allah O Akbar
I pray every morning, every day, every night
With gratitude in my heart and in my mind
God is great, God is great, God is great
The terrorist comes and hijacks this phrase of mine
Seeking Allah's help for an action not right
Allah O Akbar, Allah O Akbar, Allah O Akbar
And media picks up,
Interprets, Killer God is great!
Who is giving permission to kill the innocent?
We respond with fear, hatred and violence
Leaders rise to ban the Muslims' call to pray
Creating more chaos upon chaos
All this is happening because of our ignorance...
Allah O Akbar! Allah O Akbar! Allah O Akbar!

OCEAN OF HUMANITY
SALMA ARASTU

Do not lose faith in humanity
It is a vast, limitless, spread out ocean
It does not get dirty with a few drops of dirt at one end
Look at the sparkling waves on the other end
gushing forward to cover it!
No evil human powers can destroy its beauty
They only cry for our attention and invite us
To advance with force and dignity
Do not shake with fear at a mere bomb blast
Or several gun shots
Rise with determination like these waves
Do not stop as these are only warnings sent in lots
Move with intention to clean and heal
The naked wounds of humanity
Do not blame anyone as the evil ones are
Also part of this humanity
Designed and destined to be with us to test our humanity
Ignore them and learn to live with patience and power to heal
It is within you, O humanity
Humanity is an ocean, life-giving and eternal
Can a few drops of evil destroy this glorious unity?

LIGHT UPON LIGHT
SALMA ARASTU

When the veils of darkness disappear from your heart
You are able to visualize within,
A shimmering light!
With the glow of that light
You are able to help your friend, your neighbor
Remove dark veils of ignorance and fear
From their hearts and minds
And as they turn towards their friend
Igniting their pilot of light
My friend, that is light upon light!

ORDERS OF MAGNITUDE
SHAMIMA KHAN

Sometimes it's difficult to understand the magnitude
of God. It's like the size of the moon. It is enormous. I don't
think human beings are capable of holding the moon's size,
let alone its distance from earth, within our minds. We're so
small. We can't picture it. But the thumb of a seven-year-old
girl can cover the whole moon, depending on where she puts
her hand in the night sky. And suddenly, just like that, we can
hold out our palms, and somehow, we can reach God.

PRAYER
FAISAL MOHYUDDIN

you cleanse   the uncovered
regions   of your body
then stand   at the foot
of prayer   mats facing

the *qibla*   unfasten
your cluttered   mind
from the tangible   hold of secular
trances   bow down

before   the cascading
glow of God's mercy   submit
to a centripetal   course toward the gates
of a more perfect   emptiness

here   now
you can plunge   into the most secluded
chamber of the soul   commune
with your share   of the universe's

initial burst of   light eternal light
housed within the lamp   of mystery
waiting   to be
beheld   five times a day

BIOGRAPHICAL NOTES

Khadijo Abdi

Khadijo Abdi is a Somali American writer, poet, and former editor at Howling Bird Press. She writes about the in-between place, exploring the many intersections where people find themselves. She is currently working on her MFA thesis at Augsburg University in Minneapolis and is writing a novel about a time-traveling hijabi.

Arwa Abouon

Arwa Abouon (1982-2020) was a Libyan-Canadian artist of Amazigh descent who lived and worked for her whole life in Montreal. Earning a B.F.A. with distinction from Concordia University, she went on to become an important and greatly appreciated artist. Her work focused on issues of identity, the transmission of knowledge from one generation to another, as well as autobiographical and existential issues and, more significantly, alternative ways of seeing and being. Best-known for her large photographic works, Arwa also engaged in drawing, printmaking, film and writing. Her work is found in many private and public collections worldwide, including the Institut du monde arabe in Paris and the Montreal Museum of Fine Arts. She was also loved for her lively, brave, and empathic personality.

Barâa Arar

Barâa Arar is a community organizer and writer currently based in Toronto, Canada. She received her Bachelor of Humanities from Carleton University and is an incoming MA candidate at the University of Toronto, focusing her research on art and colonial resistance. She is a storyteller and a poetry performer who aims to give a voice to those who have been silenced or are not being heard.

Salma Arastu

Berkeley-based Salma Arastu is a painter, sculptor and poet. A native of India's Rajasthan, she has been creating and exhibiting her paintings internationally since the 1970s. Her work speaks of human universality and is influenced by Arabic calligraphy, miniature arts and folk patterns. Born into the Hindu tradition, she embraced Islam later on, enjoying the beauty of these two distinctive traditions first hand. At birth, she was given the life-defining challenge of a left hand without fingers. She has almost 40 solo art shows to her credit, and has won awards including East Bay Community Fund for Artists, 2012 and 2014, and Berkeley's Individual Artist Project Grant Award, 2014, 2015 and 2016. She has published five books of her poems and paintings. Visit www. salmaarastu.com.

@studentAsim

@studentAsim is a Canadian producer, author, filmmaker and multidisciplinary artist. He lives and works in Toronto. His work explores the meaning of Giving. @studentAsim is the author of five picture books. His fifth picture book, *The Tyer of Ties*, was published in February 2019. He is also the creator of The Champion for Life™, an artistic human progress concept, and producer of The Champion for Life™ film, which has played in film festivals internationally. Currently @studentAsim is producing an online training course for helping artists become more effective, as well as producing and raising funds for two documentary projects: the first, a historical documentary, and the second, a documentary about his father. Contact by email: *info@studentasim.com* or by twitter: @studentAsim. Visit his website at *studentasim.com*.

Leena Barakat

Leena Barakat is a Palestinian-American social justice activist, business-development professional, social impact strategist, and mother of two. She serves as the Director of Strategic Partnerships at Tides, a global philanthropic partner and non-profit accelerator, working to accelerate the pace of social change. She previously served as the Cultural Program Director at the Arab Cultural Community Center of San Francisco. She proudly serves on the Board of Directors of the Women Donors Network, funding the most critical and progressive women of color led movements of our time. She holds a Masters in Global

Development and Social Justice from St. John's University in New York and a B.A. in International Studies from the University of California, San Diego. She lives in San Francisco with her husband two children.

Sarah Basheer

Sarah Basheer is a recent graduate in communications from the University of Illinois at Chicago. She was born in the Chicagoland area to Muslim, Hyderabadi (Indian) parents who came to America in the 1990s. She is the only girl of five children. Sarah loves to write and bake, loves her black and white cat Leia, and is a massive Harry Potter fan. She loves writing because it expresses her own thoughts, opinions, and aspirations, and because it allows us to learn more about each other. She says – Writing is like feeling feelings twice, once when you first experience them and then again when you convey them to someone else and evoke the same emotions in others. Check out her personal blog: *https://herroyalhighness1.wordpress.com.*

Valerie Behiery

Valerie Behiery is a Canadian artist, writer, and academic whose life has been devoted to the arts, both their making and study. Committed to bringing visibility to underrepresented artists and convinced of the power of the arts to encourage positive social change, her writing has been published in peer-reviewed journals, reference works, art catalogues, and freelance publications like *Visual Arts News, Tribe, Nafas,* and *esse.* A global nomad, Valerie has taught at universities in Canada, Turkey, and Saudi Arabia. She is currently finishing a post-master's diploma in art therapy; having experienced the profound therapeutic effects of writing and artmaking, she seeks to help others do the same. When she has spare time, she enjoys walking, reading, and experiencing the lost art of peaceful farniente.

Halah Butt

Halah Butt was born and raised in Toronto, Canada, and her ethnicity and family background is Pakistani/Kenyan. She was raised Muslim her whole life and is proud to be one. She is currently a copywriter and editor who writes creatively on the side. She tries to write stories that capture her sense of identity as a Muslim-Canadian, stories that bring light to the current issues that society faces, and stories that give voice to those who are unable to use their own voice. When she is not writing, you can find her reading, binge-watching sitcoms, or taking pictures of trees.

Kitty Costello

Kitty Costello is a San Francisco-based poet, writing workshop facilitator, editor, and a psychotherapist with a master's degree in social psychology. She relishes writing as a tool for insight, healing, social justice and community building. She worked 30 years for the San Francisco Public Library, including 10 years driving the bookmobile to underserved communities. Her poetry book, *Upon Waking: New and Selected Poems 1977-2017,* was published in 2018. Poet friends who influenced her most include Beat Poet Diane di Prima, who taught her early on how to delve into the creative wellspring within, and Native Alaskan poet Mary TallMountain, with whom she shared the delights and transformative power of writing in community. Tai chi and chai tea are 2 favorite pastimes. Email her at *kittycostello108@gmail.com.*

Kelly Izdihar Crosby

Kelly Izdihar Crosby is a visual artist and freelance writer. She originally hails from New Orleans, Louisiana and currently lives in Atlanta, Georgia. A Muslim convert of 15 years, her faith is a source of inspiration for her art and writing. She has shown her artwork in various galleries throughout the United States and in the United Arab Emirates. She has published her work in magazines including *Azizah* and *Halal Consumer,* and she currently serves as an editorial assistant for the *Emerging Infectious Diseases Journal,* a journal published by the Centers for Disease Control (CDC). View her work and writings at *www.kellycrosbydesign.com.*

Wendy Díaz

Wendy Díaz is a Puerto Rican Muslim writer, award-winning poet, translator, children's book author, and mother of five. She is co-founder of Hablamos Islam, Inc., a non-profit organization producing educational resources about Islamic religion and culture in the Spanish language. She is the creator and voice behind Ahmed El Titeriti (Ahmed, the puppet) from the show "Hablamos Islam con Ahmed" on youtube. She is also the Spanish content coordinator for Islamic Circle of North America's *WhyIslam* and a @MuslimMatters columnist, as well as a contributor to numerous ethnic media publications. In her free time, which is almost never, Wendy enjoys reading, drawing, or watching a good movie. Read more from Wendy at *latinomuslimreporter. com* or *www.hablamosislam.com* or follow on social media @Hablamos Islam.

Ghadeer Elghafri

Ghadeer Elghafri is a Palestinian-Canadian poet, singer and actor from Gaza, born and raised in Dubai, and living in Toronto. She is a new immigrant, warrior, healer, feminist, activist and advocate and was published in *Poetry ReRooted: Decolonizing Our Tongues.* Her forthcoming chapbook is *Mad Vagina.* Ghadeer has performed in dozens of poetry nights and reads her Arabic poetry with English translation. She has organized dozens of multicultural, multilingual open mic poetry nights in the Toronto area. She is the founder and owner of Qahwa Art Café, which is a safe community performance space. Follow her on: *linkedin. com/in/gghafri, youtube.com/ghadeerelghafri, facebook.com/GhadirElGhafri, facebook.com/Qahwa-Art-Café*, Twitter: @khansaainaik @Ghadir_ ElGhafri, and Instagram: @gghafri @qahwaartcafe.

Said Farah

Said Farah is a Seattle-raised, Somali-born writer based in Minneapolis. His work engages with third-culture writers who are interested in notions of identity, displacement, and belonging. He uses writing as a way to parse the natural conflicts which arise from his multiplicities. He is an MFA candidate and graduate instructor of Creative Writing at the University of Minnesota. More of his work can be read at *www. saidshaiye.com* and he can be reached by email at *smfarah@gmail.com*.

Saba Ghazi-Ameen

Saba Ghazi-Ameen is a multimedia artist and designer living in New York and Chicago. After completing her BFA in Communication Design from UI Chicago, she earned a Master of Professional Studies degree in Interactive Telecommunications from NYU's Tisch School of Art. She has worked in both print and multimedia, designing everything from logo systems and books to interactive physical computing applications. She is active in the Maker Movement, exploring the construction and deconstruction of anything she comes across. She experiments with the intersection of visual and verbal design, taking the written word from the page to stage in open mics and poetry slams. She has performed in cities across the U.S. Find her @sabaghaziameen and *sabaameen1@gmail.com*.

Najib Joe Hakim

Najib Joe Hakim is a Political Art Fellow at the *Yerba Buena Center for the Arts* and the recipient of the 2020 Rebuilding Alliance Storytellers Award for his *Home Away from Home: Little Palestine by the Bay* project. Though not Muslim himself, Hakim has amplified the voices of many Muslims through his art projects in the Palestinian and Arab-American communities. He earned an MA in Contemporary Arab Studies from Georgetown University. His current endeavor, *Palestine Diary*, exhumes photographs he took in Palestine in 1978-79, enlightening the roots of the crisis in Palestine today.

Reem Hammad

Reem Sayem el Dahr-Hammad was born in Aleppo, Syria. When she was six years old, her family moved to Beirut, Lebanon where she grew up and studied. After getting married and moving to Los Angeles in the early Eighties, she earned a Bachelor of Fine Arts degree in Design from the University of California in LA. She worked in graphic arts and later found her passion in ceramic arts which has fulfilled her inner artist to this day. Writing is another form of self-expression for her. Joining the "Relax and Write" writing group has helped her to explore her voice and recover memories from present and past. She feels humbled to join the many talented Muslim voices in this anthology.

A. M. Hassan

A. M. Hassan is an African American convert from Buffalo, New York. She has been an avid reader and writer since childhood and enjoys writing stories about the kinds of struggles that often go untold. She is currently working on her first novel, a story that has been stuck in her heart since the age of 12. She currently lives in Ohio with her husband and beautiful daughters. Find more of her work at *amhassan88. wordpress.com*

Hanan Hazime

Hanan Hazime is a multidisciplinary artist, creative writer, community arts educator, and writing instructor living in Toronto. She also identifies as a Lebanese-Canadian Muslim Feminist and Mad Pride Activist. Hanan's writing has appeared in several publications including *The Windsor Review*, *Generation Magazine*, and *Feckless C*nt*. Awards include the Alistair & Anita MacLeod Prize in Creative Writing in 2011, and the Dr. Eugene McNamara Award for poetry in 2013. Her debut poetry chapbook *Aorta* was published by ZED Press in 2018. She's currently working on her first novel thanks to an Ontario Arts Council grant. When not writing or creating art, Hanan enjoys reading fantasy novels, over-analyzing things, photo-blogging, dancing with faeries in the woods, and drinking copious amounts of tea. Instagram: @the.mad.muslimah. Website: HananHazime.com.

Shereen Hussain

Shereen Hussain was born in India, raised in the U.K., and later moved to California. She holds degrees in French and English Literature from the University of London, and in Education from San Francisco State University. She worked as a teacher for many years, then in international business. However, writing has been a lifelong passion. She has been published in the U.K. in *Lascaux Review* and in the anthology *Happy Birthday to Me*, and in the U.S. in *Azizah Magazine*. She authored the play *Inventing the Truth*. Shereen now resides in a leafy suburb of Chicago with her family and serves on the board of the Mecca Center, where she has been involved in interfaith and outreach for over a decade. She blogs at *www.aunty-g.blogspot.com*.

Mahin Ibrahim

Mahin Ibrahim is a hijabi writer whose work has appeared in *HuffPost*, *Narratively*, and on the Muslim women website *Amaliah*, where her essay "What It's Like to Wear Hijab in the Trump Era" was the most read in 2017. In spring 2019, her essay was included in *Halal If You Hear Me*. In spring 2020, her essay "How I Found Love from My Homeless Neighbors" was included in *Fury: Women's Lived Experiences During the Trump Era*. Aside from writing, Mahin has a fondness for seahorses and beach trails. Connect with her at *mahinibrahim.com* or on twitter: @mahinsays.

Shamima Khan

Shamima Khan published her first poem at age seven and won the City of Ottawa's youth poetry award. She has published both in print and online, including on the CBC Canada site. Since 2007 she has performed her pieces as part of the annual Expressions of Muslim Women showcase and other events in Ontario. Because the media often depict Muslims, especially Muslim women, in ways that determine perceptions of them, it is important to Shamima as a Muslimah to strive for Muslim women to have a voice and to be able to tell their own stories themselves. So she writes to connect, to make sense of this world, and to let her soul transcend the confines of her skin. She believes stories are magical, spiritual and powerful.

Tehmina Khan

Tehmina Khan, a child of Indian immigrant scientists, has lived in Northern California since childhood. She has spent her adult life writing, teaching, resisting, and mothering. Tehmina has taught science to preschoolers and citizenship to octogenarians. Currently she teaches English and creative writing at City College of San Francisco, where she defends everyone's right to a quality education. Most recently, she has taught Poetry for the People classes at CCSF, where she also serves as faculty advisor to the Poetry for the People student club as well as the Muslim Students Association. She rides a bicycle, cooks spicy food, speaks multiple languages, hosts poetry events, and gathers together with family and diverse intersecting communities around the San Francisco Bay.

Ambata Kazi-Nance

Ambata Kazi-Nance is a 6th-generation Louisianan, born and raised in New Orleans. She is a writer, teacher, and editor holding master's degrees in English Literature and Fine Arts from the University of New Orleans. Raised by a Muslim father, she accepted Islam at the age of 22. Her writing has appeared in *The Peauxdunque Review*, *Cordella*, *Ellipsis*, *Blue Minaret*, and *Mixed Company*, an anthology of short fiction by women of color in New Orleans. She is writing a play about the historic Black midwife tradition and a novel about a young Muslim woman reconciling with her faith community and her identity post-trauma. Currently, she lives in Connecticut with her husband and son. Her website is *www.ambatakazinance.wordpress.com*. She muses about writing, reading, and life on Instagram @ambatakn.

Gail Kennard

A native of Los Angeles, Gail Kennard converted to Islam in the San Francisco Bay Area while attending graduate school at UC Berkeley. Today she lives in Los Angeles and leads the architectural firm her late father, Robert Kennard, founded in 1957. It is the oldest African American owned architectural practice in the western United States. Since 2010 she has served on the City of Los Angeles Cultural Heritage Commission. She is active in various Islamic, social service and interfaith efforts in Southern California. A former journalist, her writings have appeared in the *Los Angeles Times*, on the Islamicity website and other publications. She is currently writing a biography about her late father's career as an architect in mid-century Los Angeles.

Enesa Mahmic

Enesa Mahmic is a travel writer and a member of PEN Center. She has published 4 poetry collections. Her poems have been translated into 8 different languages and published in numerous anthologies, including *Social Justice and Intersectional Feminism* (Canada), *I Am Strength* (USA), *We Refugees* (Australia), *Anti-War and Peace: IFLAC Anthology* (Israel), *Global Voices of 21th Century Female Poets* (India), *Writing Politics and Knowledge Production* (Zimbabwe), *Spread Poetry, not Fear (Slovenia)*, *Le Voci della poesia* (Italy); and more. Her writing has garnered international awards: Gold Medal, *Neigbour of Your Shore 2017*, as best immigrant poem; *Ratkovic's Evenings of Poetry 2016;* and the *Aladin Lukac Award 2016* for best debut book. Raised by her Muslim family in her native Bosnia, she moved to Seattle in 2018.

Shabnam Mahmood

Born in Uganda, Shabnam Mahmood is of Indian descent and was among those expelled by Idi Amin. She now resides in Chicago with her husband, her twins, her mother, and a fish named Rumi. She is a writer, teacher, journalist, and when she is not teaching English to college freshman, she is in the kitchen cooking up a storm. She is awaiting publication of her first cookbook. Growing up in foreign cultures, it was difficult to find her voice or place in the world. Every moment is an inspiration to write. Her piece, "The Most Beautiful Place," was published in South Africa's *Jungle Jim* magazine, 2012. She contributed to Tamar Myer's *Hell Hath No Curry* and has been a staff writer for *Sisters!* and *Sahaara* magazines.

Monia Mazigh

Monia Mazigh is an academic, author and human rights advocate. She was catapulted onto the public stage in 2002 when her husband, Maher Arar, was deported to Syria where he was tortured and held without charge for over a year. She campaigned tirelessly for his release. She holds a PhD in Finance from McGill University and was a finance professor at Thomson Rivers University. She published a memoir about her pursuit of justice, *Hope and Despair*, and two novels, *Mirrors and Mirages*, stories of Muslim women in Canada, and *Hope Has Two Daughters*, about the Arab Spring. Her books have been short-listed for the Ottowa, Trillium and Champlain Book Awards. Her third novel, *Farida,* will be published in winter 2020. She regularly blogs at www. moniamazigh.com.

Katie Miranda Al Ali

Katie Miranda Al Ali is committed to illuminating beauty and truth through the mediums of painting, comics, and Arabic calligraphy jewelry. She earned a BFA and MFA in Illustration at the Academy of Art University in San Francisco. After studying Arabic calligraphy in Palestine with award winning calligrapher Ehab Thabet, she began experimenting with Arabic calligraphy jewelry. From 2005-2008 Katie lived in the West Bank and volunteered as a human rights worker with the International Solidarity Movement. Her cartoons have been published in *Mondoweiss, Middle East Eye, Middle East Monitor, Common Dreams, Dissident Voice,* and *Electronic Intifada.* In 2015 she started a nonprofit called Palbox, a quarterly subscription box featuring fair trade Palestinian crafts, organic foods, and her own jewelry. She took her shahada in 2010.

Zainab Fatima Mirza

Zainab Mirza is a Muslim from birth and was raised in Markham, Ontario, although her family is from India. She graduated from the University of Toronto with a specialization in English Literature and a minor in Film Studies. Mirza is currently pursuing a Masters in English Literature at the University of Toronto. She is also an alumna from Sigma Tau Delta, an international English honor society. Mirza believes everything is an experience a writer can pen down, and which readers can learn from; that is what inspires her to write!

Faisal Mohyuddin

Faisal Mohyuddin, the child of Muslim immigrants from Pakistan, is a writer, educator, and visual artist from the Chicago area. He is the author of *The Displaced Children of Displaced Children* (Eyewear Publishing, 2018), which won the 2017 Sexton Prize, was a 2018 Summer Recommendation of the Poetry Book Society, and received a «highly commended» citation from the Forward Arts Foundation. Also the author of the chapbook *The Riddle of Longing* (Backbone Press 2017), he teaches English at Highland Park High School in Illinois and serves as an educator adviser to Narrative 4, a global non-profit organization dedicated to fostering empathy and empowering young leaders through the exchange of stories. Learn more about him and his work at *www.faisalmohyuddin.com.*

Duraid Musleh

As a Palestinian born in the West Bank, Duraid Musleh grew up under the occupation in an activist atmosphere buzzing with literature, lectures, discussions and revolutionary poetry. With so little work in the West Bank, he left in 1978 to study in Jordan, then Holland, then the U.S., earning multiple master's degrees in engineering and computer science, eventually settling in Silicon Valley and working in the software industry. He is a lifelong activist who stays connected to the Palestinian community in the U.S. and back home, feeling camaraderie with others who understand the frustrations of occupation and displacement. He is a calligrapher and a poet who composes mostly in Arabic. Love and Palestinian affairs are his primary themes.

Samar Najia

Samar Najia is an Arab American, born in Lebanon. Her parents were made refugees during the mass exodus of Palestinians in 1948 (also known as the *Nakba*, meaning Catastrophe) and subsequently the civil war in Lebanon in 1976. The family migrated to several countries before settling in the U.S. She graduated from Georgetown University and currently works for an international bank. She is presently writing a memoir about a middle-class Palestinian family's journey from refugee to citizenship. Her focus is the unresolved sense of loss and statelessness that clings to the psyche of the Palestinian refugee, though she is inspired by the shared courage and resilience of refugees worldwide. The memoir is in mixed prose and poetry form. Samar is married with two sons.

Kristen Obarsky

Kristen Obarsky is an eclectic writer who experiments with various styles and genres. She currently lives in wonderful Minnesota, but was born in Pennsylvania's dynamic hills where she lived her early years. She later relocated to Indiana's vast countryside and graduated from Indiana University with a Bachelor of Arts in Biology and Anthropology. She found an unexpected passion as a homeschooling educator. As a Muslim convert and homeschooling educator, she found a concerning lack of literature and materials representing Muslim voices and is motivated to fill those gaps. When she is not writing or teaching, she delights in making colorful abstract paintings. Her current published works include: "The Minnesota Wild, a Swirl of Sensations and a Taste of Minnesota Nice," *Star Tribune*, 2018, and *letterstothebeloved.com*.

Abdul-Malik Ryan

Abdul-Malik was born Michael Park Ryan in Chicago, Illinois. His study of African-American history in high school and at DePaul University and his encounter with the life and legacy of Malcolm X led to his accepting Islam in 1994. He was a founding member and past president of the board of directors of the Inner City Muslim Action Network. He graduated from Georgetown University Law Center and worked as an attorney for children in the foster care system in Chicago for 14 years. He has served as an imam and chaplain since 2009. In addition to Islamic theology and law, he is passionate about interfaith dialog and Irish history and culture. He currently lives in the south suburbs of Chicago with his wife and their five children.

Maryam Sabri

Maryam Sabri is 9 years old. She's a 3rd grade student in Margot Pepper's class at Rosa Parks Elementary School in Berkeley, California. She loves sea turtles and Italian food. She plays on a girls' basketball team at the YMCA called the Flaming Marshtatoes. Maryam loves to travel and has been to Paris, León, and throughout Tunisia and the United States. She wants people to think of Tunisia with the same fondness they think of France. When she grows up, she wants to be a traveler and explorer who writes and photographs her experience. Currently, she is writing her own travel book with her friend Anica. This is her first published work.

Tayyaba Syed

Tayyaba Syed is the award-winning author of the children's picture book *The Blessed Bananas*. Her writings and bylines have appeared in numerous publications such as *Encyclopedia Britannica*, *NPR*, *Chicago Parent* and *Islamic Horizons*. She volunteers for Daybreak Press (the publishing arm of a women's nonprofit called Rabata), teaches writing, leads a weekly women's *halaqa*, and performs readily as a fun storyteller. She worked as the Creative Developer for *Noor Kids* educational books and as a co-author for the *Jannah Jewels* chapter-book series. She has conducted more than 100 literary presentations from the U.S. to Qatar and Turkey. Tayyaba is pursuing her Islamic Studies certification through the Ribaat Academic Program and lives with her husband and three children in Illinois. Learn more at *tayyabasyed.com*.

Aquil Virani

Awarded as the "Artist of the Year" by the Quebec-based artist collective "Artists for Peace," Aquil Virani is an Indian and French Ismaili Muslim visual artist and writer living on unceded territories of the Kanien'kehá:ka (Mohawk) Nation in so-called Montreal, Canada. He exhibited *Canada's Self Portrait* at the Canadian Museum of Immigration and premiered his *Postering Peace* documentary at the Aga Khan Museum. He is currently working on a commemorative portrait series honouring victims of the Québec City Mosque Attack in collaboration with the victims' families. His latest project, *CelebrateHer,* is a large-scale feminist portrait series and sound play collaboration with Erin Lindsay and Imago Theatre, supported by the Canada Council for the Arts (*celebrateher.ca*). Learn more at *aquil.ca.*

Zainab bint Younus

Zainab bint Younus is a Canadian Muslim woman whose passion for reading led her to writing at a very young age. She was first published at age 14 in a local Muslim community newspaper in Vancouver, and later, at age 16, she became a co-founder, writer, and editor for MuslimMatters.org. She has also written for *SISTERS Magazine, Al Jumu'ah Magazine, AboutIslam,* and the *Huffington Post.* Her fictional story, "Not a Love Story," was published in the anthology *Habibi.* In her daily life, Zainab is a chocolate-selling ninja, a slightly beleaguered madrasah teacher, and the mother of a sometimes-too-clever girl. She can be found online at her blog: *http://phoenixfaithandfire.blogspot.com.*

Hanaa Walzer

Hanaa Walzer reverted to Islam in 1994 while finishing her undergraduate studies at Acadia University in Nova Scotia. She then obtained an MA in Languages and Literatures from the University of Ottawa and a PhD in Hispanic Studies from McGill University in Montreal. She was born in Canada but was raised in Switzerland by her Swiss father and Mi'kmaq mother, along with her two siblings. She has lived on four different continents and currently resides in Canada with her husband and their four children, after leaving Libya due to the ongoing conflict. She has published both academically and in leisure magazines, and works as an educator. She also continues to write and edit freelance through her site *www.hanaasediting.blogspot.com* and maintains a lifestyle blog at *www.cafecaterpillar.blog.*

GLOSSARY

This glossary provides English translations of most non-English words used by the authors. We have left the transliteration choices up to each author, so you will sometimes find various transliterations for the same word, such as saree *and* sari. *Authors have also used various ways of translating, opting for either the letters or the actual pronunciation, for example,* al-Rahman *or* ar-Rahman *respectively. We have intentionally retained these diverse usages, both in the text and in the glossary.*

abaya (Arabic) – a full length outer garment worn by some
    Muslim women

al-Amin (Arabic) – the Trustworthy; one of the nicknames given to
    Prophet Muhammad

Alhamdulillah (Arabic) – All praise and thanks are due to God.

Allah ya Rahman (Arabic) – Oh Allah the Most Compassionate

Allah, ar-Rahman, ar-Rahim (Arabic) – the first 3 of the 99
    names of God in Islam: Allah, the Most Compassionate,
    the Most Merciful

Allah O Akbar or Allahu Akbar (Arabic) – God is the Greatest
    (for Muslims, a reminder that God is greater than the beauty
    and ugliness of this world.)

Alshukrulillah (Arabic) – All thanks be to God.

al-watan (Arabic) – the motherland

Ameen or Amin (Arabic) – How you say Amen in Arabic.
    Used at the end of prayers and supplications to God.

anarkali (Urdu) – a long, flowing, woman's dress-like garment;
    literal translation is "pomegranate flower"

ansar (Arabic) – "the helpers," the local inhabitants of Medina who
    took Muhammad and his followers into their homes when
    he emigrated from Mecca

as salaam 'alaykum or Assalamu alaykum (Arabic) – Peace be
    upon you. This is how Muslims greet each other.

a 'uthu a'uthu billaahi min ash-shaytaan ar-rajeem (Arabic) – I
    seek protection in Allah from the accursed Satan.

Ayaat (Arabic) – an Islamic girl's name meaning "signs"

Barakallah (Arabic) – The blessings of Allah.

bint al-Quds (Arabic) – daughter of Jerusalem

Bismillah, ar-Rahman, ar-Rahim (Arabic) – In the name of Allah, the Most Compassionate, the Most Merciful

breek or brik (Arabic) – North African savory filled pastry, often deep-fried

buraq (Arabic) – a mythical creature in Islamic tradition, said to be a horse-like transport for certain prophets

centre d'achat (French) – shopping center

choti (Urdu)– braid

dadi (Urdu) – grandmother

deen (Arabic) – religion; literally means the way of life Muslims adopt to comply with divine law

dépanneur (French) – convenience store

dépaysement (French) – scenery

désolé (French) – sorry

dhikr (Arabic) – a form of verbal devotion in which the worshipper is absorbed in the rhythmic repetition of the names of God or His attributes; literally means simultaneously remembering and intoning

duga or duqqa (Arabic) – an Egyptian condiment consisting of a mixture of herbs, nuts, and spices

Eid (Arabic) **or Eid al-Fitr** – Festival of Breaking the Fast that marks the end of the month-long dawn-to-sunset fasting of Ramadan

fajr (Arabic) – dawn; the fajr prayer is the 1st of the 5 prayers Muslims perform daily

fatwah (Arabic) – a legal opinion or ruling issued by an Islamic scholar

Fi Amanillah (Arabic) – May Allah protect you.

ghulaam (Arabic) – a servant boy in paradise

hadith (Arabic) – a narrative record of the sayings and customs of Muhammad and his companions; they constitute the second source of guidance for Muslims after the Qur'an.

hajj (Arabic) – the annual Muslim pilgrimage to Mecca, that all Muslims are expected to make at least once during their lifetime

halal (Arabic) – permitted in Islam; or more specifically, denoting or relating to meat prepared as prescribed by Muslim law

hamam (Turkish) – public bath (*hammam* in Arabic)

haveli (Urdu) – a traditional townhouse or mansion in India or Pakistan, usually one with historical or architectural significance

hijab (Arabic) – a head covering worn in public by some Muslim women

hijabi (Arabic) – a woman who wears hijab

Iblees or Iblis (Arabic) – a *jinn* mentioned in the Qur'an

iftar (Arabic) – the evening meal for breaking the fast at sunset during the Islamic month of Ramadan

inshallah or insha'Allah (Arabic) – God willing

in situ (Latin) – left in the original place

isha (Arabic) – Islamic night prayers; the 5th of the 5 daily prayers Muslims perform

Islam pour toujours (French) – Islam forever

Ismaili (Arabic) – a member of a specific branch of Shia Muslims

jamaat (Arabic) – the broader Ismaili community

Je ne veux pas que nos enfants grandissent dans la peur (French) – I don't want our children to grow up in fear.

jenna (Arabic) – paradise; heaven

jinn (masculine) **or jinniyyah** (feminine) (Arabic) – supernatural creatures in early pre-Islamic Arabia and later Islamic mythology and theology; "genie" is the Anglicized form of the word.

Jumu'ah Mubarak. (Arabic) – Have a blessed Friday.

kahwa or qahwat (Arabic) – coffee

keffiyeh (Arabic) – a Bedouin Arab's kerchief worn as a headdress

khana kao (Hindi) – eat

khateebah (Arabic) – sermon giver

khoja (Hindi) – Ismaili Muslims originating specifically from India
(as opposed to Afghanistan, Syria, or elsewhere)

khutbah (Arabic) – sermon

Khudhahafiz (Persian) – May God be your guardian/protector, a
common parting phrase.

Khushyali (Hindi) – an Ismaili celebration

kibbeh (Egyptian Arabic) – a Middle Eastern dish of ground lamb
with bulgur wheat and seasonings

kichari or kachdi (Hindi or Bengali) – a dish from the Indian
subcontinent made from rice, lentils and spices

kilim (Turkish) – a flatwoven rug (or prayer mat)

kufi (Arabic) – a brimless cap worn by many populations in
Africa and Asia, often worn by Muslim men during the
5 daily prayers

La ilaha illa Allah. (Arabic) – There is no god but God.

La terre est à tout le monde. (French) – The earth belongs
to everyone.

L'union fait la force. (French) – Unity is strength.

madrassa (Arabic) – any type of educational institution,
secular or religious

majnoon (Arabic & Persian) – crazy; also the name of a character
from an old story of Arabic origin, who was crazily in love

Mashallah (Arabic) – What God has willed; used to express
appreciation, joy or praise for what has just happened.

masjid (Arabic) – mosque

merguez (Arabic) – sausage

minbar (Arabic) – pulpit

mubaraka (Arabic) – holy

Muslima (Arabic) – a Muslim woman

nabi (Arabic) – a prophet

nakhla (Arabic) – palm tree

naseeb or nasib (Arabic and other languages) – destiny; fate

Non au racisme. No al racismo. (French, Spanish) –
No to racism.

Nos larmes ont le meme gout, notre sang, la même couleur.
(French) – Our tears have the same taste, our blood,
the same color.

Nous faisons tous partie de grande famille de l'Humanité.
(French) – We are all part of the great family of Humanity.

On apprécie beaucoup le soutiens des non musulmans.
(French) – We greatly appreciate the support of
non-Muslims.

qibla (Arabic) – the direction of the Kaaba (the sacred building at
Mecca), to which Muslims turn at prayer

Qur'an (Arabic) – the Islamic sacred book, believed to be the word
of God as dictated to Muhammad

poutine (Canadian French) – a dish of French fries topped with
cheese curds and gravy

Ramadan (Arabic) – the 9th month of the Islamic (lunar) calendar,
a holy month of fasting, introspection and prayer for
Muslims (fasting is one of the 5 pillars of Islam).

rasul (Arabic) – an Islamic messenger or apostle;
a given name or surname

resistance contre la violence (French) – resistance
against violence

Sadaqah Jaariyah (Arabic) – continuous charity; ongoing
charitable acts that continue even long after one has
passed away

sadiq (Arabic) – truthful

Sahabiyaat (Arabic) – the great stories of the female companions
of Muhammad

Salaam (Arabic) – Peace; a shortened salutation used to say hello
and goodbye

Salaam alaykum (Arabic) – Peace be upon you.

saree or sari (originally from Sanskrit) – a women's garment from
the South Asia, typically wrapped around the waist, with
one end draped over the shoulder

shahadah (Arabic) – the Muslim declaration of belief in the oneness of God and the prophethood of Muhammad; one of the 5 pillars of Islam

shakshuka (Arabic, Hebrew) – poached egg in spiced sauce; literally, "all mixed up"

shalwar kameez (Persian and Urdu) – traditional South and Central Asian dress that is a combination of trousers and tunic

Shia (Arabic) – one of the two main branches of Islam

subhanahu wa ta 'ala (Arabic) – the most glorified, the most high

Sunni (Arabic) – the larger of the two main branches of Islam

surah (Arabic) – a chapter in the Qur'an (there are 114 surahs in the Qur'an)

Surah al-Jinn (Arabic) – Chapter of the Jinn, the title of the 72nd chapter of the Qur'an

tahfiidh or tahfiz (Arabic) – the act of memorizing

tamer (Arabic) – dates

tasheeh (Urdu) – rectification; a correction or revision to a text; the process of making a correction or revision to a text

teen or tayn (Arabic) – fig

terre d'ouverture (French) – land of openness

thobe or thawb (Arabic) – a long tunic worn by men, especially in Arab States of the Perisan Gulf and some parts of Egypt; a garment of modest attire for men

ulemaa or ulema or ulama (Arabic) – a body of Muslim scholars recognized as having specialist knowledge of Islamic sacred law and theology.

ummah (Arabic) – the whole community of Muslims bound together by ties of faith

Un Québec libre est un Québec uni (French). – A free Québec is a united Québec.

Vous êtes mort dans les bras de Dieu (French) – You died in the arms of God.

wa 'alaykum as salaam (Arabic) – and peace be with you; the response to assalamu alaikum

zatar or zaatar (Arabic) – a mixture of spices named after thyme,
the main ingredient, combined with toasted sesame seeds,
dried sumac and other spices

zayt (Arabic) – oil such as olive oil

zaytouna (Arabic) – olive

HAPPY WRITING

Contact the editors at *muslimamericansathome@gmail.com*.

CPSIA information can be obtained
at www.ICGtesting.com
Printed in the USA
JSHW040333240321
12837JS00002B/129

9 780915 117321